The Missional Leader

The Missional Leader

Equipping Your Church to Reach a Changing World

Alan J. Roxburgh and Fred Romanuk

Foreword by Eddie Gibbs

A Leadership Network publication

Published by Jossey-Bass
A Wiley Imprint
989 Market Street, San Francisco, CA 94103-1741 www.josseybass.com

Library of Congress Cataloging-in-Publication Data

Roxburgh, Alan J.
The missional leader: equipping your church to reach a changing world / Alan J. Roxburgh and Fred Romanuk; foreword by Eddie Gibbs.
p. cm.—(Leadership network series)
Includes bibliographical references and index.
ISBN-13: 978–0–7879–8325–3 (cloth)
ISBN-10: 0–7879–8325–X (cloth)
1. Mission of the church. 2. Church growth. 3. Church. 4. Missions. I. Romanuk, Fred. II. Title. III. Series.
BV601.8.R69 2006
266—dc22

2006000723

Printed in the United States of America
FIRST EDITION
HB Printing 10 9 8 7 6 5 4

Leadership Network Titles

Leading from the Second Chair: Serving Your Church, Fulfilling Your Role, and Realizing Your Dreams, by Mike Bonem and Roger Patterson

The Way of Jesus: A Journey of Freedom for Pilgrims and Wanderers, by Jonathan S. Campbell with Jennifer Campbell

Leading the Team-Based Church: How Pastors and Church Staffs Can Grow Together into a Powerful Fellowship of Leaders, by George Cladis

Organic Church: Growing Faith Where Life Happens, by Neil Cole

Leading Congregational Change Workbook, by James H. Furr, Mike Bonem, and Jim Herrington

Leading Congregational Change: A Practical Guide for the Transformational Journey, by Jim Herrington, Mike Bonem, and James H. Furr

The Leader's Journey: Accepting the Call to Personal and Congregational Transformation, by Jim Herrington, Robert Creech, and Trisha Taylor

Culture Shift: Transforming Your Church from the Inside Out, by Robert Lewis and Wayne Cordeiro, with Warren Bird

A New Kind of Christian: A Tale of Two Friends on a Spiritual Journey, by Brian D. McLaren

The Story We Find Ourselves In: Further Adventures of a New Kind of Christian, by Brian D. McLaren

Practicing Greatness: 7 Disciplines of Extraordinary Spiritual Leaders, by Reggie McNeal

The Present Future: Six Tough Questions for the Church, by Reggie McNeal

A Work of Heart: Understanding How God Shapes Spiritual Leaders, by Reggie McNeal

The Millennium Matrix: Reclaiming the Past, Reframing the Future of the Church, by M. Rex Miller

Shaped by God's Heart: The Passion and Practices of Missional Churches, by Milfred Minatrea

The Ascent of a Leader: How Ordinary Relationships Develop Extraordinary Character and Influence, by Bill Thrall, Bruce McNicol, and Ken McElrath

The Missional Leader: Equipping Your Church to Reach a Changing World, by Alan J. Roxburgh and Fred Romanuk

The Elephant in the Boardroom: Speaking the Unspoken About Pastoral Transitions, by Carolyn Weese and J. Russell Crabtree

Contents

About Leadership Network

Since 1984, Leadership Network has fostered church innovation and growth by diligently pursuing its far-reaching mission statement: to identify, connect, and help high-capacity Christian leaders multiply their impact.

Although Leadership Network's techniques adapt and change as the church faces new opportunities and challenges, the organization's work follows a consistent and proven pattern: Leadership Network brings together entrepreneurial leaders who are focused on similar ministry initiatives. The ensuing collaboration—often across denominational lines—creates a strong base from which individual leaders can better analyze and refine their own strategies. Peer-to-peer interaction, dialogue, and sharing inevitably accelerate participants' innovation and ideas. Leadership Network further enhances this process through developing and distributing highly targeted ministry tools and resources, including audio and video programs, special reports, e-publications, and online downloads.

With Leadership Network's assistance, today's Christian leaders are energized, equipped, inspired, and better able to multiply their own dynamic Kingdom-building initiatives.

Launched in 1996 in conjunction with Jossey-Bass (a Wiley imprint), Leadership Network Publications present thoroughly researched and innovative concepts from leading thinkers, practitioners, and pioneering churches. The series collectively draws from a range of disciplines, with individual titles offering perspective on one or more of five primary areas:

1. Enabling effective leadership
2. Encouraging life-changing service
3. Building authentic community
4. Creating Kingdom-centered impact
5. Engaging cultural and demographic realities

For additional information on the mission or activities of Leadership Network, please contact:

Leadership Network
www.leadnet.org
(800) 765-5323
client.care@leadnet.org

Foreword

by Eddie Gibbs

The past few years have witnessed a plethora of books addressing the challenges facing the church in the midst of profound cultural transition. These titles, addressing the situation of the churches in the West, are set against a backdrop of persistent church decline experienced by most, if not all, of the traditional denominations. Some of these books have focused on the cultural context, providing evidence that the changes taking place at least during the past four decades are deep-rooted and comprehensive. They have an impact on every institution, including government, business and commerce, the military, education, and health care.

The church is not immune to the loss of confidence in our human ability to come up with solutions to fundamental problems relating to the environment, a growing world population, the purported clash of civilizations, and a technological revolution that has advantaged the privileged (who both contribute to and benefit from scientific advances) over those who are excluded from enjoying the benefits (through lack of education and work skills). All this is within a global context and amid fear of terrorism that has created a climate of uncertainty. Along with leaders in every other institution, church leaders are overwhelmed by the flood of facts, theories, and opinions let loose in this information age; they experience a loss of place amid increasing pluralism and the prevailing culture of relativism.

There were also, especially in the 1970s and through the 1990s, a spate of books from leaders of megachurches, whose growth has bucked the general trend. They trumpeted a message of success, inviting other leaders to adopt their methods in order to achieve similar results. Their expectations were seldom realized. It appears that the impressive growth of many megachurches was in fact mostly at the expense of other churches. This raises the question as to what their future will be once they have drained the pool dry. Yet they must not be so readily dismissed, because some of these large churches have made a significant contribution in reactivating lapsed church members by offering a worship experience and need-based ministries. These offerings established their relevance to a constituency that left out of boredom or frustration.

Then we have seen still other books that perceive the missionary challenge and gospel opportunity of the present state of uncertainty. They call for a new kind of church, envisioning one that is far less hierarchical, much more mobile, and outwardly focused. They emphasize the need to move from a church shaped over many centuries by the dubious assumptions of Christendom. Such churches operated on a come-to-us basis, in which the surrounding community is invited into the worshiping community on its terms.

This model too has now passed its "sell-by" date in most locations. It needs to be replaced by a missional model of church, one that is outgoing and expressed in countless local initiatives. This is the church of the first two and a half centuries of its existence, as recorded in the New Testament and by the Apostolic Fathers, before the conversion of Emperor Constantine. It is also the kind of church that is experiencing such phenomenal growth in Africa south of the Sahara, in Latin America, and parts of Asia. These churches, which are the fruit of missionary initiatives from the West, are in turn reaching out to the West and contributing increasingly to revitalizing the old Churches of Europe and North America, and to evangelizing those who have abandoned the church—or never ventured through its door.

A growing number of church leaders are beginning to catch the vision of another kind of church. Some of these leaders are to be found within traditional denominations, which is where the authors of this volume work, primarily as consultants. Others are arising within independent initiatives, which either stand alone or establish links with wider networks. These networks themselves birth new faith communities. But these emerging churches are not clones of existing ones, a process that characterized so much of the church planting endeavors of past decades. Rather, they are based on a missional understanding of church that emphasizes an incarnational, servant approach and sees church not as a once-a-week gathering but as a community to which one belongs that relates to the whole of life. It is a community in which each person makes an active contribution, during gathered worship as well as dispersed service. These churches emphasize hospitality and are therefore small. They are small not because of their limited appeal but because they are committed to maintaining their values of community, accountability, and service, and to being reproducible on an exponential scale. This is indeed an inspiring vision.

The challenge for so many church leaders, whether or not they have received formal training, is that they are not equipped to lead such a church. They were trained to pastor and teach in an existing church context to the satisfaction of its members. Our training models are conditioned by a Christendom mind-set and the agendas of the academy. As a consequence, we neglect the three other areas of ministry listed first in Ephesians 4, all of which are of crucial importance in the missional church: the gifts of apostle, prophet, and evangelist. (As one Australian denominational executive lamented, "We are suffering from a dire shortage of APEs!")

To break out of such a shrinking, we need the entrepreneurial leader who can birth new faith communities. We need the prophet who has learned the discipline of listening to God and is able to impart a clear vision and discerning counsel. We need the evangelist who can commend Christ with grace and authority and equip local churches to communicate the good news as a choral statement.

The frequently heard cry of church leaders who have captured the vision is, "How do we transition from a consumer model of church to one that is essentially missional in nature?" Or, "How do we birth such a church, when we have never had the opportunity to be involved in one?"

This is where the present volume makes a unique contribution. It is the first book I have come across that addresses, in a very practical way, how to make the transition. It identifies the critical issues that every leader must consider before beginning the process and then offers wise counsel on how to navigate the process, giving frank recognition to the fact that the passage will almost certainly be stormy, disruptive, and disorienting. This is not a book of quick fixes and slick slogans, but one that sets out a comprehensive and in-depth treatment. Some books can be mastered in one read. This is the kind of volume that leaders will want to return to again and again as they face fresh challenges. The insights contained in these pages are a timely guide not only for the paid staffs of churches but for their entire leadership team, to afford mutual understanding and a common vision. Alan Roxburgh and Fred Romanuk draw on years of experience as church consultants, and their insights are now made available to a much wider audience. I am convinced they will make many more grateful friends as a consequence.

Eddie Gibbs
Donald A. McGavran Professor of Church Growth
School of Intercultural Studies
Fuller Theological Seminary
Pasadena, California

Introduction

The question is familiar: "What do you mean by missional church?" Even though the term is now used everywhere, there is still confusion about it. As we begin this book, here is a brief description of what we mean by the phrase.

God is about a big purpose in and for the whole of creation. The church has been called into life to be both the means of this mission and a foretaste of where God is inviting all creation to go. Just as its Lord is a mission-shaped God, so the community of God's people exists, not for themselves but for the sake of the work. Mission is therefore not a program or project some people in the church do from time to time (as in "mission trip," "mission budget," and so on); the church's very nature is to be God's missionary people. We use the word *missional* to mark this big difference. Mission is not about a project or a budget, or a one-off event somewhere; it's not even about sending missionaries. A missional church is a community of God's people who live into the imagination that they are, by their very nature, God's missionary people living as a demonstration of what God plans to do in and for all of creation in Jesus Christ.

The Missional Leader

PART I

The Context and Challenge of Missional Leadership

CHAPTER I

Six Critical Issues for Missional Leadership

ALAN WAS LEADING A WORKSHOP AT A YOUTH Specialties/Emergent conference in San Diego. The group comprised some one hundred church leaders from all kinds of churches—experimental, long-standing, mainline, and congregational. But from all the groups the common question was, "How do we lead and form these missional/emergent congregations you keep talking about? How do we form missional congregations without blowing up the churches we're serving, or losing our job?"

This book is written out of the conviction that *we need a new approach to leadership for missional communities.* We come away from countless encounters with pastoral teams and denominational executives with the pressing sense that the tools and resources they are using will not address the critical issue of forming missional communities of the Kingdom in a time of rapid, discontinuous change. We believe there are six critical issues in developing a missional leadership in our day.

Issue One: Missional Leadership Is *the* Key—But How Do You Do It?

There's a lot of good theological and biblical conversation going on about creating missional churches and communities, but little sense of or assistance for how such leadership can actually be developed. Alan was sitting in the office of a denominational executive talking about the church's need for change. This executive had read the book *Missional Church: A Vision for the Sending of the Church in North America.* He turned to Alan and said, "I love this missional theology. I believe in what you folks are saying. The critique of culture, the evaluation of the church and the theology are wonderful. But what do I do with it? Pastors come into my office asking me for help. And I know that just giving them 'how-to' programs isn't going to help them.

"But neither is this book. It's too academic. Most of my pastors will read it and have no idea what to do with it at the end (if they understand it at all). You see, when a pastor walks into my office and asks for help with other kinds of issues or problems, I can reach onto my shelf and pull off any number of programs that will help them know what to do. But this missional conversation is just that: it's a conversation, but there's nothing to help us know how to do it in the real life of our congregation."

At the end of a workshop at a convention for emergent leaders, a similar thing happened. This time it wasn't a denominational executive but a young pastor in an experimental congregation in the Midwest who said, "Al, what you're saying about the church and our culture is absolutely right! It resonates with my heart. I was feeling excited and energized as you spoke. But where does someone like me go to learn how to be this kind of leader?"

Alan didn't have an answer for him. Leaders are eager to engage in the missional/emergent conversation, but their most pressing questions suggest they're struggling to make sense of how to actually lead in this new way after they go back home.

Issue Two: Most Models Repackage Old Paradigms

In response to demand, numerous books are being published with missional language in the title. What is disappointing about most of these books is that they use missional language to repackage the familiar language of church effectiveness, church growth, and church health. In other words, the writers have not engaged the nature of the change a missional paradigm requires and are simply offering a few more good tactics for doing the same thing more effectively. Leadership models are borrowed from psychology (counselor, therapist), medicine (health and healer), the business world (strategist, coach, manager), and the educational world (teacher). A lot of congregations and leaders have been socialized to view these models as the only viable ones. A denominational executive told us about one extreme but real example. He met with a congregation of about 150 people. Describing the profile of the new pastor they wanted, they told him they were not interested in anyone wanting to bring about change. They wanted their church to be like a hospital with a pastor who looked after their needs and metaphorically changed their IVs when required. This is a pastor-medical model of leadership, and it is based on palliative care. It may be extreme, but it is a sign of the borrowed cultural images that shape our understanding of church and our expectation of leaders. The executive admitted that although this was a gross example of a church's pastoral search, it was not far from what many actually wanted.

In another case, a congregation called us to ask how it could remove the current pastor because she wasn't an effective change agent. The job description they developed called for an entrepreneurial leader who could make things happen—clearly a business model. Both examples demonstrate that the leadership models currently shaping the church are inadequate to forming a missional church. In their own context and setting—medicine, the business world, counseling—these images of leadership are appropriate, but when the church borrows and applies such models to the community of God's people it misses an opportunity to shape leadership around the biblical sense, in which leadership is about cultivating an environment that innovates and releases the missional imagination present among a community of God's people. What do we mean by the language of "environment"? We use the word in much the same way as we would say we want to create an environment that enables our children to thrive. In other words, what are the skills, capacities, and habits that we as parents would want to cultivate that give our children all the things they need to thrive? When we talk about the water quality of a lake, we seek to describe those elements in the water that contribute to the fish in the lake thriving, or making sure that what we put into the lake as human beings helps to maintain high-quality water for drinking and swimming. In other words, we cannot *make* our children into what they will become, just as we cannot make water in that sense. But in both cases we can, as parents or responsible citizens, set the context for the child or the lake to thrive as it should. In the same way, missional leadership is about creating an environment within which the people of God in a particular location may thrive.

Issue Three: Discontinuous Change Is *the* New Norm

At a meeting with a dozen executive staff members of a denomination, we heard one, reflecting on the dynamics of the congregation, say that she felt every time she turned around things changed. The executive responsible for resourcing Christian education spoke up: "The very nature of change has changed, but I can't quite get my mind around this discontinuous-change idea. How is it different from continuous change?" After a while, another executive looked at his associates around the table and said, "The reality is that discontinuous change has become the new continuous change, and we were never trained to deal with this kind of world!" Everyone nodded in agreement. It's a new kind of world!

We heard similar sentiments from an executive leader of a major denomination in a series of three-day meetings concerning some critical issues of innovation in the denomination. We had just brought to this group of some thirty people a comprehensive report (based on about one hundred exhaustive interviews from across the system) on the primary issues confronting its congregations and leaders. The executive looked over the report, sighed, and said: "I'm just plain tired of all this change; I don't have energy left to address it all anymore!" After a pause, he smiled and said, "But I know these are accurate descriptions of what we're facing, and I know I need to address the new changes!"

Almost every book one picks up these days and most conferences on leadership begin with the same theme: our culture is in the midst of rapid, extensive transformation at every level. We are moving through a period of volatile, discontinuous change. Change is always happening; that's not the issue. There are two kinds of change we want to consider in this book: continuous and discontinuous. Let us illustrate the difference between these two types of change.

Continuous change develops out of what has gone before and therefore can be expected, anticipated, and managed. The maturation of our children is an example. Generations have experienced this process of raising children and watching them develop into adults. We can anticipate the stages and learn from those who have gone before us how to navigate the changes. We have a stock of experience and resources to address this development change; it is continuous with the experience of many others. This kind of change involves such things as improvement on what is already taking place and whether the change can be managed with existing skills and expertise.

Discontinuous change is disruptive and unanticipated; it creates situations that challenge our assumptions. The skills we have learned aren't helpful in this kind of change. A friend became the executive vice president for finance in a college at quite a young age. One day, just before Christmas and about a year into the job, he returned from a fundraising trip and was immediately invited into the president's office. He assumed it was for a regular meeting, but he discovered a member of the board in the room as well. The president passed a letter across his desk to the young VP and told him not to go back to his office; there was a career counselor waiting to see him because his job in the institution was over right then and there. This friend found himself suddenly in a world he never anticipated and for which he had no coping skills. In discontinuous change:

- Working harder with one's habitual skills and ways of working does not address the challenges being faced.
- An unpredictable environment means new skills are needed.
- There is no getting back to normal.

Discontinuous change is dominant in periods of history that *transform* a culture forever, tipping it over into something new. The Exodus stories are an example of a time when God tipped history in a new direction and in so doing transformed Israel from a divergent group of slaves into a new kind of people. The advent of the printing press in the fifteenth century tipped Western society toward modernity and the pluralist, individualized culture we know today. Once it placed the Bible and books into everyone's hands, the European mind was transformed. There are many more examples, from the Reformation to the ascendence of new technologies such as computers and the Internet, that illustrate the effect of rapid discontinuous change transforming a culture.

Discontinuous change and developmental change are not the same. Developmental is about more of what has been; it's change within a familiar paradigm. Examples are everywhere. One buys a new car or introduces drums or drama or video into a worship service; a book written about missional leadership has a familiar chapter on the need for high commitment to church membership rather than asking the deeper questions of membership and belonging. These instances are all about change *within* a world. They don't address the deeper, underlying issues. The skills and competencies for leading this kind of change are learned by habit and training within the system. Thus the churched culture of the twentieth century said to aspiring leaders, "If you want to be a pastor in this denomination you must go to Seminary X and learn skills Y and Z; then you will be ready. We know skills Y and Z are the right ones because they have worked well in the past and will continue to serve us into the future."

For more than a century, North American churches were at the center of culture; they were an essential part of most people's belief and value systems. Therefore, leadership skills and capacities were developed around how to most effectively engage people when they came to the church. It was about training men and women who would faithfully run effective branch plants of the denomination so that when people came they would be well served with a set of expected resources, experiences, and programs. Leaders who ran these churches really well grew in prestige, respect, and influence.

Discontinuous change is different. There is a wonderful IBM ad that captures something of what it means. A team of people evidently starting up a business, after working hard to develop an online marketing strategy, gather around a computer as their product goes online. They look hopefully and expectantly for the first Internet sale. When one comes through, they nervously look at each other, relieved that something has happened. Then ten more sales come through.

Muted excitement runs through the anxious room. Then, suddenly, a hundred or so orders show up on the computer screen. The team is cheering and hugging one another in exultation; all their hard work has paid off. Then they stare at the screen, beyond disbelief: instead of hundreds of orders, which they couldn't have imagined in their wildest dreams, there are suddenly thousands. Everyone is overwhelmed. No one knows how to deal with this; it's outside their skills and expertise. They are at a loss to know what to do next. The organization has moved to a level of complexity that is beyond the team's skills and ability to address.

In a period of discontinuous change, leaders suddenly find that the skills and capacities in which they were trained are of little use in addressing a new situation and environment. What do congregational leaders do when the skills that have been effective in drawing people in and building it up no longer get the same results because the growing numbers of emerging generations are no longer interested in being attracted into a church building or joining the church programs?

Issue Four: Congregations Still Matter

Despite the claim that congregations are so hopelessly compromised they cannot make the adjustments required to missionally engage our new context, a congregation can become a center of missional life.

We are not naïve about the challenges. Many congregations are in significant decline. For a lot of people, the congregation is little more than a haven in a heartless world, a dispenser of religious goods and services to individuals. Nevertheless, it is still populated by the people of God. God chooses to create new futures in the most inauspicious of places. Through the Incarnation, we discover that God's future is at work not where we tend to look but among the people we write off as dead or powerless to make things different. If the Spirit has been poured out in the church—the church as it is, not some ideal type—then we are compelled to believe that the Spirit of God is at work and alive among the congregations of America. Congregations matter. But they need leaders with the skills to cultivate an environment in which the Spirit-given presence of God's future may emerge among the people of God.

Issue Five: Leaders Need New Capacities *and* Frameworks

A denominational executive sits listening to a group of pastors share their convictions about the shaping of a missional church for their denomination. His arms are folded across his chest, his legs crossed, as he listens in silence. His body language suggests nervousness and resistance; yet, like a good leader, he has chosen to come to this meeting and listen to these men and women share their hearts with him. A veteran of many years, he has given his heart to his denomination and gotten many a bruise from his efforts. He knows the statistics, just like everyone else. This once-proud mainline denomination is bleeding members every year, budgets are plummeting, reserves are running low, and the remaining staff are being obliged to carry more and more work. Something needs to be done.

After the pastors finish speaking, his initial comments reveal the needling questions he brought with him. He is concerned that he seems to hear a lot of negative things from the missional church movement. From his perspective, missional church seems to be telling him that he what he did in the past was wrong, that he and others just don't know how to lead in this new world. He is concerned about the criticism of his and his peers' leadership.

This executive is both right and wrong. He and his peers are exemplary; they lead with excellence and great skill. The skills and capacities that shaped church leadership for much of the twentieth century were the right ones for that context. We are not critiquing these skills and capacities. Our point is that the world has changed. Discontinuous change means that many rules and assumptions about leadership now need to be reexamined and rewritten. This does not make those who have led us in the past wrong; it means we are functioning in a different context. Just as a missionary who moves from North America to another culture must unlearn a lot of habits and skills to learn how to be present and effective in a way that achieves results in the new context, so we pastors and denominational leaders in North America are now in a place where we must *all* learn new capacities if we are to achieve effective missional results.

The important point to remember is that we are all in this situation together. We are all learners on this journey. This is not a matter of judging or accusing or dismissing the past efforts of leaders of great skill, passion, and integrity. All of us in leadership, young and old, experienced veterans and raw recruits, must discover together the new shape of leadership.

The classic skills of pastoral leadership in which most pastors were trained were not wrong, but the level of discontinuous change renders many of them insufficient and often unhelpful at this point. It is as if we are prepared to play baseball and suddenly discover that everyone else is playing basketball. The game has changed and the rules are different.

The situation requires cultivation of new leadership capacities. Alongside the standard skills of pastoral ministry, leaders need resources and tools to help them cultivate an environment for missional transformation. In one congregation, a staff of five pastors struggled to deal with complex, multiple expectations they had of themselves and the congregation had for them. They could articulate what was meant by a missional ecclesiology, and they had read several books on missional church, but they struggled with conflicting images of what it means to lead and what the congregation expected. They articulated what was for them a helpful way of describing their situation using a summary chart analyzing what they believed were two different paradigms operating both in them as leaders and in the congregation (see Table 1.1). We're not suggesting this is the correct description of the divergent expectations and roles, only that it's illustrative of what we believe is actually happening among leaders in the church today.

The Pastoral Model in Table 1.1 represents, for them, the role expectations placed on or held by congregational leaders. Here the assumption is that people come to the church to receive religious goods and services, and the pastor is, like a priest, present to engage and meet their spiritual or religious needs in every way. This team believed that the image described under this column continues to be the more dominant and powerful model, both for pastors and those who attend church. When they looked at the Pastoral Model, they readily admitted that most of the skills in which they were trained were developed for functioning in this framework. They clearly understood that for a large percentage of the congregation pastoral care is still a central competency for any leader of a congregation. But this team also recognized that it is no longer a sufficient skill set for leaders. Simply

TABLE 1.1. *Operating Models of Leadership.*

Pastoral	*Missional*
Expectation that an ordained pastor must be present at every meeting and event or else it is not validated or important.	Ministry staff operate as coaches and mentors within a system that is not dependent on them to validate the importance and function of every group by being present.
Ordained ministry staff functions to give attention to and take care of people in the church by being present for people as they are needed (if care and attention are given by people other than ordained clergy, it may be more appropriate and effective but is deemed "second-class").	Ordained clergy equip and release the multiple ministries of the people of God throughout the church.
Time, energy, and focus shaped by people's "need" and "pain" agendas.	
Pastor provides solutions.	Pastor asks questions that cultivate an environment that engages the imagination, creativity, and gifts of God's people in order to discern solutions.
Preaching and teaching offer answers and tell people what is right and wrong. • Telling • Didactic • Reinforcing assumptions • Principles for living	Preaching and teaching invite the people of God to engage Scripture as a living word that confronts them with questions and draws them into a distinctive world. • Metaphor and stories • Asks new questions
"Professional" Christians	"Pastoring" must be part of the mix, but not the sum total.
Celebrity (must be a "home run hitter")	
"Peacemaker"	Make tension OK.
Conflict suppressor or "fixer"	Conflict facilitator
Keep playing the whole game as though we are still *the* major league team and *the* major league players. Continue the mythology that "This staff is the New York Yankees of the Church world!"	Indwell the local and contextual; cultivate the capacity for the congregation to ask imaginative questions about its present and its next stages.

TABLE 1.1. *Operating Models of Leadership, Cont'd.*

Pastoral	*Missional*
"Recovery" expert ("make it like it used to be")	Cultivator of imagination and creativity
Function as the manager, maintainer, or resource agent of a series of centralized ministries focused in and around the building that everyone must support. Always be seen as the champion and primary support agent for everyone's specific ministry.	Create an environment that releases and nourishes the missional imagination of all people through diverse ministries and missional teams that affect their various communities, the city, nation, and world with the gospel of Jesus Christ.

being skilled at caring for people once they come to the church is not sufficient for engaging the changing context in which a congregation finds itself.

The Missional Model they developed (Table 1.1) represented, for them, the emerging leadership paradigm they wanted to innovate in the congregation. This model recognizes a context in which people have an ever greater variety of religious options. A congregation must become a place where members learn to function like cross-cultural missionaries rather than be a gathering place where people come to receive religious goods and services. As the team articulated this list, they were aware that they needed a whole new set of leadership skills.

You may choose your own description and categories, but the principle is the same: in a situation of rapid discontinuous change, leaders must understand and develop skills and competencies to lead congregations and denominational systems in a context that is missional rather than pastoral.

Issue Six: *A* Congregation Is *a* Unique Organization

A congregation is not a business enterprise and cannot be treated as such. But this is precisely what most books and programs for innovating missional life in congregations are doing. They tend to borrow their ideas and strategies from the latest processes in the business world and merely use so-called missional language to describe what is being proposed. The denominational systems that came into their own in the twentieth century were modeled after and came to look like North American corporate organizations. But a congregation is not a business organization, nor is it meant to be run like a minicorporation through strategic planning and alignment of people and resources around some big plan. The congregation comprises the people of God, called to be formed into a unique social community whose life together is the sign, witness, and foretaste of what God is doing in and for all of creation. Just as early Christian communities chose nonreligious language to express this unique new life (using the overtly political word *ecclesia*), so the church today must understand again its calling as the missional people of God. The calling does not require borrowing language and structures from secular organizations but rather formation of a unique imagination as a social community of the Kingdom.

The habits and activities of many congregations and leaders seem disconnected from the purposes to which God calls the church in North America today. We need to imagine the forms and structures of church life in this situation that are not simply uncritically borrowed from other systems. A leader must be able to help a congregation:

- Understand the extent to which strategic planning and other such models misdirect the church from faithful witness in our culture
- Create an environment wherein God's people can discern for themselves new forms of life and witness
- Thrive in the midst of ambiguity and discontinuity

Even though the regular operational or administrative functions of a congregation continue to require attention, they must now support other leadership skills: cultivating the missional imagination of the people of God in the midst of massive change. This book introduces those skills and presents a framework for understanding why they are important and how they can be applied.

CHAPTER 2

Cultivating the Imagination of the Missional Leader

FOR A LONG TIME, WE DIDN'T RECOGNIZE WHAT was happening among a lot of church leaders, but one day in a meeting of a group of pastors who had been together for about six months, meeting each month for a full day, we were struck by a realization. Their executive was coaching the team around issues of skills and competencies for leading missional change, and they were working through a reflection process to identify a primary missional leadership challenge they would address in their congregation. The next step would involve a meeting the following day with some eighty lay leaders from their combined congregations.

One of the pastors in the group saw a board member on the street shoveling snow from the sidewalk. He rushed out to see whether this board member would be at the meeting the next day. When the pastor returned a few minutes later, he had a crestfallen look on his face. "See, that's what it's like around here!" he exclaimed. "I just went out to check if Jim was coming to the meeting tomorrow, and he said to me, 'Pastor, I'm not interested in that stuff; I won't be there.'" The pastor was clearly discouraged, and not by just this one incident. He pointed out how most of his leaders had the same attitude. They would promise to participate but come only if there really wasn't anything better to do.

There was a murmur of agreement around the room. As the conversation continued about what had just happened, we were struck by the depth and pervasiveness of the malaise the group was feeling. Most of these pastors had come to a place of believing that nothing could change in their congregation. Although they met month by month to look at their leadership skills and talk about missional leadership challenges, they had not been able to recognize or address a much deeper issue that sat with them around the table: they hardly believed God could or would do anything new among their people or under their leadership.

This malaise does not affect just pastoral leadership; it extends to many congregations as well. A good friend once said that the most important currency a congregation has to spend is hope. If it gets spent down, there isn't much of anything else left. In many congregations the hope account is low and the cupboards of hope are getting bare. People have tried programs and worked through schemes over and over again but have seen little substantive change. This drains their hope. Like their pastor, a congregation can lose hope and cease to believe that the Spirit of God is among them. They mouth the words of belief but in reality it's a long-lost wish.

Without addressing this malaise among leaders and congregations, there will be little innovation in missional life. The culture of belief and expectation in which these leaders and congregations are operating needs to be changed. What follows are some of the signposts for addressing this change. They are drawn and shaped from a biblical and theological narrative that shapes a Christian understanding of how God is at work in the world. It is important to note that the basis for the proposals in our book is these signposts, not prior assumptions and models of leadership drawn from other disciplines and practices. This is not to deny the importance of role models from other sources in innovating missional leadership, but the basis for all our thinking and acting needs to be a biblical and theological imagination.

Cultivating *a* Biblical Imagination

The narrative imagination of Scripture challenges our assumptions about what God is up to in the world and reminds us that leaders can do great things when they align their expectations with God's. An important role of a missional leader is cultivating an environment within which God's people discern God's directions and activities in them and for the communities in which they find themselves. The biblical narratives are full of stories about places and people without hope who become centers of the Spirit's creative, world-changing activity. This can still be the case. For congregations and leaders who feel they can't compete, keep up with, or emulate the examples of growth and success held up for them at conference after conference, this is exuberant, life-giving news. These stories demonstrate not some optimistic wishful thinking but a conviction about the God we encounter in Jesus. We, like the people in these biblical stories, are invited to cultivate our imagination to see the possibilities of what the Spirit wants to do in and among the people we are called to lead. The biblical narrative suggests to us some key elements of missional leadership.

The INCARNATION

Missional leaders take the Incarnation of Jesus with the utmost seriousness. More than just a doctrine to be confessed, it is the key to understanding all God's activities with, through, in, and among us. It points toward an answer to the question of where God is to be found. In the Incarnation we discern that God is always found in what appears to be the most godforsaken of places—the most inauspicious of locations, people, and situations. God seems to be present where there is little or no expectation. A group of slaves, gypsies wandering around the edge of civilization, become pathetic brick makers for an empire. These nobodies of the earth, like all the other unnamed, no-name peoples before them, were about to disappear from the face of the earth in yet another Shoah. Their first-born males were being killed off as an expedient form of population control. When the cries of these slaves came to God's ear, God claimed them as his people and determined to free them from bondage and misery.

The narrative continues as this no-name people receive a new name from the One who came down to wrestle with their forefather Jacob. Centuries later, the offspring of these slaves are defeated by another mighty empire and held in abject captivity in Babylon. Again, in the Godforsaken Babylon (the name itself bespeaks the absence of God), they encounter God and their world is changed. An old man, past hope, keeps the light of the temple in Jerusalem. His wife is an embarrassment because she is far past the age of childbearing and there is no son. Yet God comes to these two elderly faithful people, and their world is transformed. A young girl, just a teenager, in an obscure village becomes pregnant with the life of God. Over and over again, God meets God's people with the bright light of the Kingdom in what appears to be the most hopeless and forsaken places.

In these biblical narratives God is constantly present in places where no one would logically expect God's future to emerge, and yet it does, over and over. There is nothing in these stories about getting the wrong people off the bus and getting the right ones on to accomplish great ends and become the best organization in the world. This God who pursues us is always calling the wrong people onto a bus that isn't expected to arrive. The reason for all of this is that God chooses, within the mystery of God as the Other who cannot be described and confined within the schemes and imagination we develop, to unfold the future of the kingdom among people and places of this kind. The vision of Ezekiel is a commentary on this whole movement of God. The Jewish Scriptures end with the books of the Kings, which in many ways is a rather dark and bleak ending. A part of that ending is a haunting question asked by God in a vision: "Can these dry bones live?" In reality the question isn't answered until Jesus appears as the one who is God's enfleshed presence among people. God's answer to the question is God himself: Jesus the Incarnate Lord, who comes among us in the most unexpected and inauspicious times and places.

We encounter many congregations and church leaders functioning out of low expectation and hope. Many leaders are giving up on existing congregations in the misguided belief that there is no hope among the established ones. Younger leaders want to go off and plant in order to start anew, while older leaders yearn for retirement or a move. But the Biblical stories that lead to the Incarnation keep telling us these are the very places where God's future emerges. This is what God does and how God acts, most clearly in Jesus. When leaders bring this imagination to their congregation, they foster hope. But this is just the beginning of the story. To all who boldly declare that the congregation has no future in an emergent, postmodern world, the biblical imagination has another response.

The Spirit *of* God *Among the* People

Many would say that congregations are becoming little more than an idiosyncratic relic shaped by quaint memories of a fading past. We were invited to attend a one-day conference on the future and the church. One of the leaders said in the morning session that we needed to "liquidate" institutions and buildings; he then went on to contrast the "institutional" church with what he called the "organic." It was clear, despite protestations to the contrary, that there was a strong sense that existing congregations didn't have much relevance to God's future. This speaker from elsewhere had clearly not indwelt the Biblical narrative very much. We are not prepared to write congregations off. We realize that some have declined and dwindled to the extent that the greatest gift they can give to the Kingdom is to close and offer their assets to others to journey forward. However, many congregations are not in this situation. We say this not because they are filled with all the right people with all the right stuff. On the contrary, dispirited people populate many congregations. They have no idea what to do in the face of loss, decline, and a radically changed world. Nevertheless, if God's Spirit is among the people of God, wherever they are (including in congregations), then these are the places where it is possible to incarnate a missional life. As with the struggles of Israel, this kind of missional transformation is costly and requires hard work.

God's Future *Among* God's People

It may sound obvious to say that God's future is among God's people, among congregations, but it's not. What does it mean to say that God's future is among God's people? In John chapter 20, a group of disciples is locked away in a room. They are terrified of the authorities, fearing that they too will be arrested and put to death like Jesus. They've lost hope and are looking for a way out. They are an assorted group of Galileans, hangers on, and women—the nobodies of the world. They are without hope. Suddenly, Jesus enters the room and stands among them. They are stunned and confused because he did not come through the door. Most of them believe he is dead, despite rumors and reports from the women. Jesus shows them his hands and sides, the solid physical tokens that prove he is the one put to death on the cross but now standing before them. Then he speaks a word into the room: "Shalom!" At first blush it might sound as if he is trying to calm their fears, almost like a gentle greeting. But the rest of the passage suggests John, in writing this Gospel, believed that Jesus is up to something far more significant than pastoral care designed to create a soothing environment. These are men and women schooled in their Scriptures. They know, in this captive land under Roman occupation, that *shalom* means far more than simply, "Be at peace and don't get too upset!" Jesus is speaking the language and longing of all the prophets and poets of the Jewish Scriptures for the day that will come when God's future, God's Kingdom, comes among them to end exile and usher in a new era. The language of *shalom* in this context is answering God's questions in Ezekiel about the dry bones. In that locked room, among a bunch of nobodies without hope, Jesus announces that this promise has come to be among them. God's future comes toward us, and it is embodied in this group of frightened people.

The rest of the passage shows that this ushering in of God's Kingdom is Jesus' intention. After speaking, he turns to the disciples, breathes on them, and declares, "Receive the Spirit." This act of breathing coupled with the announcement takes them back into their imagination, shaped by the narrative memory of their Scriptures to another time and another act of God. Jesus' action and words are a recapitulation of the creation story in which God takes the mud of the earth, breathes into its matter the Spirit (*nephesh*), and creates humanity. In other words, right in that room—right among this bunch of frightened nobodies who have no hope—Jesus constitutes the new humanity. Here is where the church is born. Look at the ordinary people Jesus begins with; this is consistent with how God has always chosen to act. Then to this new humanity Jesus gives new instruction, to go and announce the Kingdom.

What is present here is literally that in God's economy the Spirit is among the people of God. Therefore the answer to the question "What does it look like to be God's people in this strange new place?" is found among the ordinary men and women in congregations across North America. God's future is among the regular, ordinary *people of God.* It's not primarily in great leaders or experts but among the people, all those people most leaders believe don't get it. This insight leads to one more characteristic that runs steadily through the Biblical narratives.

God Turns Up *in the* Most Godforsaken Places

As we have pointed out, God is always turning up in the most forsaken of places. Throughout Scripture God's future comes from the bottom up in the most unlikely people and places. Imagine the people and places with the least potential, and there is where God's strange future is likely to be found. Turn to Abram, to Israel about to die in Egypt, to a Gentile woman named Ruth, to a remnant in exile, to an old man keeping his turn in the Temple in Jerusalem where he's told a son named John will be born to his aged wife. Turn to a teenage girl named Mary, to a Cross, and to a band of unlikely men and women who just don't get what is happening as they hide behind locked doors. Here, in all these unlikely places, is where God's future bursts forth to change the world.

Today, we give up on congregations that we declare are out of touch with the culture. We run to big, successful places with marquee-name leaders to find out how to be successful. In so doing we are going in exactly the opposite direction from everything we see in the Biblical narratives. We have forgotten that God's future often emerges in the most inauspicious places. If we let our imagination be informed by this realization, it will be obvious that we need to lead in ways that are different from those of a CEO, an entrepreneur, a super leader with a wonderful plan for the congregation's life. Instead we need leaders with the capacity to cultivate an environment that releases the missional imagination of the people of God.

Organizational Culture *and* Missional Leadership

Congregations are organizations, and like every other organization that has ever existed they form their own particular kind of culture. The organizational culture of a congregation can either hold it back from cultivating a missional life or give powerful assistance in discovering how to innovate missional life. Organizational structure in itself will never get us to the place of becoming a missional community, but it can act as a wonderful vehicle for the journey.

Sometimes people resist talk about a congregation's organizational culture because they believe it focuses on management tactics and omits the work of the Spirit. Michelle, a lay leader we met, was frustrated when she wrote in an e-mail, "But where's Jesus in all this stuff? If you have no Jesus then it's just one more piece of worldly information that I'm not interested in!" Like many others, Michelle's division of the worldly from the spiritual reveals a limited understanding of the Incarnation. In Jesus, all of life is taken seriously and becomes the realm of God's actions.

In his dispute with the Pharisees over the appropriate way of keeping the Sabbath as well as the rules and expectations they laid on ordinary people in terms of their religious responsibilities, Jesus revealed how good people had become enmeshed in an organizational culture that blinded them to God's work. Their institutionalized practices and convictions created a culture that kept them from seeing Jesus as they eagerly sought God's purposes. The same thing happens in congregations. Organizational culture shapes how we think about and see the world. Forming a missional community requires asking hard questions about the organizational culture of our congregation.

"Why Can't They Learn Like *the* Rest *of* Us Had *to*?"

Over time, organizational culture tends to develop an assumption in its members that the way it operates is the way things ought to be. An organizational culture that begins as a life-giving form can become a barrier to seeing and adapting to the challenges of a changing cultural context. Alan tells a story about his family just after they immigrated to Canada from Liverpool, England. His mom, who was in her fifties when they came, was born, grew up, married, and had her children literally in the same house and on the same street in Liverpool. She seldom left the neighborhood that was her whole world. It had its own forms of belonging and its special language, Scouse, that only those inside it understood. Then the family immigrated to Canada. The shift was so huge that she might as well have gone to the moon.

At that time, Canada was in a periodic cycle of debate about being a nation of two official languages, French and English. The controversy was how much French language education students outside of Quebec should be given and to what degree the civil service across the country should be bilingual. Alan's mom did not understand the issues because she read the world through her life in Liverpool. As the family sat around the lunch table watching the news, the children tried to explain to her the notion of two founding nations and the requirement of two official languages. She looked at them and said, "Why can't the *&#!@ French just learn English like the rest of us had to?" She wasn't aware of what she'd just said. She was talking out of her own experience in a specific, narrow culture in Liverpool, England.

We are all formed in environments or cultures that shape how we interpret the world. The Pharisees wanted to love God, but their environment shaped them such that they missed the story of God's presence in Jesus. The same is true for congregations. Without understanding how their organizational culture shapes them, members of a congregation will ask their version of why others can't learn English the way the rest of them had to.

Changing Culture, Changing Congregations

The rapid change in the world around us makes a lot of us feel like immigrants in a new land. Our cultural context is now filled with a plethora of new images, needs, demands, expectations, and attitudes that result in many feeling deeply disconnected from the present situation. People are less interested in the traditions and programs shaped by people raised in a church culture. A younger generation views organizations and institutions as an impediment to their creativity. These same young adults are shaped less and less by notions of a family church and more by the associational relationships displayed by the TV program "Friends." They are more connected with a program like "Lost," with its group of rootless strangers, than any notion of a long-term community of tradition and loyalty. People are no longer willing to learn the internal language of the congregation. They are not shaped by loyalty to institutions and have little interest in joining groups or programs. No amount of rearranging of programs will change this. The reality is that the organizational cultures, the environments, created in congregations over several generations are no longer able to engage the changed context and its emerging generations. This is why so many congregation members feel as though they are immigrants in their own culture. Things have changed so much in such a short time. Missional leaders need to do a couple of things to form missional communities.

Discern God in Change

Missional leaders must learn how to discern what God is doing in, through, and among all the movements of change in which a congregation finds itself. To do this, leaders will develop the capacity to assist the members in reflecting on what they are experiencing, and listening to each other's stories in terms of their encounter with a radically changing environment. This involves more than simply talking about what is happening in the church. In fact, quite the opposite: it involves discerning ways of unfolding the narratives that run deep inside people and yet have not been given words for many of them. We discuss this in more detail in a moment.

For too long, congregations have focused on organizational techniques for attracting people into their life and growing their numbers. There is nothing wrong with these desires, but the focus assumes we already know what God is up to among those in the congregation and in our community, so that all we need are techniques to attract others into the congregation. Missional communities are discovering that this is not the case. They are learning they need to listen and discern again what is happening to people in the congregation and in the community, and then ask these questions: What is happening to people? What might God be saying in the stories and narratives of the people in a congregation, if we would listen to them and give them voice? In what ways might God already be ahead of us and present among people in our community? How might we join with God in what is already happening?

One of the church communities we are in conversation with has begun discovering this way of life. Several of the members would drive themselves and their children to a large church some twenty minutes from their home. Along with this they taxied their children to a multitude of church programs and events without being aware that they hardly ever spent time with the people in the church who lived close to them in their neighborhood. This couple gradually became aware that their church life reflected their larger life, filled with activities and business, shaped by oughts and demands with little sense of connection and belonging.

This awareness came to light during yet another stressful car ride to another meeting and program. They began to meet with other Christians in their neighborhood rather than drive to programs all over the city. They asked each other about what was happening in their lives, the sense of being driven by forces out of their control, their hunger for belonging but having neither the time nor the capacity to develop it. In the midst of these questions, they engaged Scripture and began asking what was happening in their own community and neighborhood.

This was not an easy journey. In fact, it was profoundly difficult and took them many months that moved into several years. But gradually a new sense of being God's people emerged as they engaged their community, worked with others in town, and began shaping projects for the creation of welcoming connections in the town. The details of what they did are another story. The point here is that they learned to ask profoundly different questions about being God's people; these questions came out of their willingness to listen to the stories that were really shaping and determining their lives. Their work is about how leaders can create an environment that assists people in discerning what God is up to among them.

Create Culture in a Congregation

Missional leaders understand and develop the capacity to innovate new *culture* within a congregation. In *Leadership Without Easy Answers,* Ronald Heifetz makes a helpful distinction between *organizational change* and *cultural change.* A simple example illustrates this distinction. Organizational change occurs when leadership seeks to change the structures of the small group ministry in the church. This can be done by adding new insights about group dynamics, or another formula for putting groups together in terms of people mix, or a new kind of group process based on the latest studies and research. All of these are useful and helpful ways of restructuring and reshaping group life in a congregation. But what they miss is that research on small groups in congregations indicates that the focus of the vast majority of small groups is on the self or the needs of those in the group. Again, that is not a bad thing, but the focus of energy and attention of small group life in congregations is still on care and resourcing of the self and others. What is not the center of focus and energy of a small group is God.

Cultural change looks at how to create a small-group environment in which the focus of group attention shifts from the self and one another to God. This cannot be achieved with new structures or study guides and group dynamics. It requires a completely new set of skills and capacities. This is the kind of direction we discuss in this book because missional church is not about new techniques or programs for the church. At its core, missional church is how we cultivate a congregational environment where God is the center of conversation and God shapes the focus and work of the people. We believe this is a shift in imagination for most congregations; it is a change in the culture of congregational life. Missional leadership is about shaping cultural imagination within a congregation wherein people discern what God might be about among them and in their community.

Old *and* New Models *of* Leadership

As we discussed in Chapter One, the dominant metaphors of leadership in our time[1] have been either pastoral (caring for the flock of God, counseling, and spiritual care) or entrepeneurial (the leader who knows where the church needs to go and has the vision, passion, and strategy to take it there).

Leadership as Caretaking or Entrepreneurship

The pastoral model in its contemporary practice is not actually derived from New Testament models of the pastor. In its current usage, the word has been directly shaped (and redefined) by the fields of psychology and therapy as well as by modernity's focus on the self and the expressive individual. The pastor is thus primarily a caregiver, a spiritual counselor who looks after the private, personal, inner spiritual needs of individuals who choose to contract in and out of relationships as they do or don't meet their needs. This imaginative framework shapes our understanding of pastoral leadership. Pastoral leadership as an identity that participates in forming an alternative society of God's kingdom has been largely abandoned in favor of the caregiving identity. In a time when individuals are rapidly disembedded from primary social relationships, where their level of anxiety and insecurity grows, it is natural that people look for those who will care for them and offer a haven in a heartless world. But this should not be mistaken for the calling to form communities of the kingdom.

Even though the caregiving pastoral model of leadership has been dominant, it is being rapidly displaced by an entrepeneurial model. Whole systems of church life are being formed on the basis of the CEO leader who takes charge, sets growth goals, and targets "turnaround" congregations, much like a business CEO who comes in to lead a failing corporation. This narrative is deeply rooted in the North American myth of the heroic, charismatic personality who, like some form of spiritual superman or superwoman, guarantees success through the power of personality or strategic skill. As congregations face decline and recognize that their ways of going about being church are not reaching people, demand for this kind of leader grows and will continue to grow in the face of the anxiety and confusion that many congregations are experiencing.

In this book we offer an alternative model of the missional leader who is a *cultivator* of an environment that discerns God's activities among the congregation and in its context. It is leadership that cultivates the practice of indwelling Scripture and discovering places for experiment and risk as people discover that the Spirit of God's life-giving future in Jesus is among them.

Leadership as Cultivation

Cultivation as a metaphor for leadership does not imply that congregations are simply waiting around for someone to put them into groups where they can suddenly solve the challenges of mission and identity they confront. No one is that naïve. The idea of leadership as cultivating an environment is difficult to grasp because of our ingrained conviction that leadership is about providing solutions and strategies with predefined ends. Rather than the leader having plans and strategies that the congregation will affirm and follow, *cultivation* describes the leader as the one who works the soil of the congregation so as to invite and constitute the environment for the people of God to discern what the Spirit is doing in, with, and among them as a community.

The notion of the leader as a bigger-than-life individual not only fills the movies but is deep in our Western imagination. Such notions have contributed immensely to the malaise of leadership in congregations and to the loss of any functional belief that God has given to congregations all they need in order to thrive as a foretaste and witness of the kingdom.

Plato's famous cave allegory perhaps explains why we are so captured by this heroic myth of leadership. In this allegory, there is a cave in which people are chained in leg and neck irons so that they can look only directly at the wall in front of them. Behind, out of their sight, is a bonfire. Between the fire and the people is a puppeteer with figures whose images and movements are reflected as shadows on the wall in front of the people. The captives falsely believe that the shadows are reality. A few captives, through great hardship, break free from their chains and arduously climb out of the cave into the light. Initially blinded by the sun, they gradually grasp what reality is about and return to the cave to lead others out of captivity and ignorance.

Applied to leadership, Plato's allegory is a flawed understanding of the people of God that views them in a disturbing way. It projects profound mistrust of the ordinary and everyday. Its message is that no hope can come from those ordinary men and women bound in the cave; they are captive to blind forces beyond their control.

The biblical naratives tell another story. God encounters us in the ordinary and everyday. What we experience in the ordinariness of life is not a shadow but the reality of God's world and God's presence. We may have become blinded to the wonder of the ordinary and what God is doing in its midst, but it is not some liberated individual climbing to a mountain top who brings new sight. It is the Spirit of God in Jesus who causes all people to see in new ways as they enter the Kingdom. Leadership is not about enlightenment but cultivation of an environment that releases the missional imagination of God's ordinary people. Enlightenment is about special knowledge that the ordinary world and its people cannot have. But the Incarnation puts an end to this gnostic, Platonic idealism. Jesus' birth stories tell us that God and God's future meet us—in the ordinary and everyday.

Another serious consequence of this Platonic myth is its dependency on self-assertion by the heroic, in which an overcoming individual strives to make his or her own world independent of God. It is in the end about Nietzsche, not Christ.

In this heroic myth, ordinary people and ordinary life are reduced to the level of slavery and ignorance. People cannot discover things for themselves but must be led to knowledge or understanding by a heroic leader. Is it any wonder congregations believe the leader must have the answer, solution, and plan? In this view, leaders by definition have seen the truth in ways that ordinary people never can. The only ones who know what is going on are the experts trained in certain ways; all others are "laity," people bound in the chains of everyday life.

Sociologist Zygmunt Bauman points out how this view of ordinary people in ordinary life was present in the birth of the modern social sciences. Commenting on the perspectives of sociology's founding fathers, Max Weber and Emile Durkheim, Bauman describes "an underyling agreement between them on at least one point: individual actors are not good judges of the causes of their own actions, and so their individual judgments are not the stuff of which good sociological accounts of 'social reality' can be made, and are better left out of account. What really makes individuals tick, including their genuine, not self-assessed, motives, is located in the world outside and more often than not eludes their grasp."[2] Therefore only experts and professionals see the light well enough to lead others. This conception has dominated church assessment of leadership in recent times as much as it has informed ideas of secular leadership. This is why it is so immensely difficult to shift to a model of leadership as cultivating environments. Congregations themselves no longer believe they have among them the God-formed resources to discern and shape the future God calls them to embrace.

As we have emphasized already, the fallible, often compromised, congregation is the unspectacular and insignificant place where God's Spirit brings forth the unexpected; it is in these social communities that the missional future will emerge. Paul said it wonderfully in 1 Corinthians when he described the meaning of the cross. He confessed that God had not chosen the powerful or the rich to build the kingdom; rather, "God chose the foolish things of the world to shame the wise; God chose the weak things of the world to shame the strong. He chose the lowly things of this world and the despised" (1:27–28). God chose those things that are not (the very people and places we have already decided are useless and need to be discarded because they are useless, dead containers of the past) to confound what is and to form the new future of the Kingdom. There is no better description of the congregation today, no better description of what many leaders have concluded about their people. The amazing, counterintuitive reality of the One we meet in Jesus is that God enters the ordinariness of our confused congregation and its organizational system. God enters among people who don't get it, who are often compromised beyond hope, and there God calls forth new imagination. Christian imagination is about announcing that God does a new thing by entering into the very real places where we are formed, to transform them. This is what the Incarnation is about; this is what greets us on Easter morning in the resurrected Jesus. It is also true of the church (see Ephesians chapter 1). Those who want to discard and give up, throw away and start again with a clean slate, have no understanding of the biblical drama, the meaning of the resurrection or God's heart. Missional leadership must be about cultivating the capacity and gifts of the people who are already part of the church.

When people understand leadership as cultivation, a new excitement about the possibility of congregational life emerges. A pastor in Los Angeles, trained at a prominent evangelical seminary, said she had at last encountered a way of leadership that filled her with hope and made her want to return to church again. Instead of the burden of leader as superhuman person, leadership as cultivation opens a space to discover ways of forming the missional community.

Three Elements *of* Leadership *as* Cultivation

Cultivation takes time and involves the rhythms and cycles of life. It cannot be rushed or made to happen. Cultivation is an art as well as a skill; it requires new habits, skills, beliefs, and attitudes. There are four important elements involved in this process of cultivation.

Cultivating Awareness and Understanding

The missional leader requires skills to cultivate three new kinds of awareness in a congregation. First is the awareness of what God is doing among the people of the congregation. John and his family had been part of the church community for several years. He was viewed as a capable leader who could play an important role. But when asked to serve on boards and committees or lead a small group, he consistently said no. Over coffee one day, Bill, a friend and leader in the church, asked John about his decision not to participate in leadership. It was only then that a picture emerged. John was a highly paid engineer in a successful design company, but the growing level of outsourcing was threatening his job as well as those of the people under his direction. This threat was causing great tension in John as he struggled to figure out how to put his two children through college and work through potential scenarios of job change. His church community afforded no environment for John or others to talk about the real issues confronting their lives. It was only by chance that another leader managed to hear the points of anxiety—the very points at which God's future is discerned.

Second is awareness of how a congregation can imagine itself as being the center of God's activities. An associate pastor was giving a teaching series on the values and mission of the congregation. It was a mixed congregation, economically and culturally. One morning the pastor was talking about the mission of the church as a welcoming community in its neighborhood. What she pointed out in particular was that this church community should welcome refugees who were coming into the neighborhood. The pastor happened to live in a project that offered hospitality and residence to refugees, which was a wonderful calling. But that morning she made it clear that the role of the church as a whole in fulfilling its mission of welcoming should be to do this. She was taking her firm commitment to an expression of welcoming the stranger and making it normative for all. Again, this kind of "ideological ought" for everyone in the congregation misses what is happening among people and therefore misses what God is up to among people. In this particular case, many people in the congregation are struggling to make sense of their lives as young families subjected to economic forces that seem destructive to meaningful community life. Many of these people want to understand and discern how to form alternative ways of living as God's people in a time when it is unclear how to do so. Here is an amazing opportunity for listening to what is happening among God's people and creating a context for dialogue, rather than telling people what and where they should be spending their time and energy.

Third is an awareness of what God is already up to in the congregation's context. This requires a capacity for listening to and engaging the images, narratives, and stories of people with plenty of stress, anxiety, and confusion in their lives and world that keep morphing and leave them struggling to make sense of what was once familiar, comfortable, and manageable. Take voluntarism as an example. Robert Putnam's *Bowling Alone in America*[3] shows that the voluntarism that enabled churches to thrive has all but disappeared as members come under increasing economic and work pressures. People are increasingly disconnected from one another as social structures that once connected them break apart.

Cultivating Colearning Networks

To create an environment that releases the missional imagination of a congregation, leaders need to cultivate forms that give people space to experiment and test out actions with one another. Such a *colearning network and community* fosters ways for church members to discover together new habits for missional life. A network involves developing loosely connected teams that learn together how to experiment with new ways of engaging their community and neighborhood and with new ways of engaging Scripture as well as having conversation with one another.

For example, in one Midwestern church we encountered the congregation recognized it had entered a long slide into mediocrity. The great days of fifteen to twenty years earlier were over; the church's neighborhood was in rapid transition. People filled positions with little sense of how to address the congregational challenges they faced. Clergy leaders were confused about what to do. They saw that their people were wrestling with a changing world, job insecurity, and the painful loss of younger generations from church life. The programs and activities that once worked for them failed to address the malaise.

In response, the congregation formed a series of lay-led teams to look at the issues they faced. The leadership of the congregation went through their own learning process, where we assisted them in understanding that if God's Spirit was genuinely among the people of the congregation then the role of leadership was to create an environment that would call forth God's imagination for the church at this point in time. The leadership understood; they believed this was right but acknowledged they had no idea how to cultivate such an environment. We worked with the leadership over several months, helping them understand some of the principles for cultivating action and vision from among the people.

The specific method we used was a process designed around what we call missional action teams. Over a number of months, the leadership identified key areas in the congregation's life where these teams might be formed to address critical challenges to mission. They formed several teams and began to discern new ways of creating a missional environment in the congregation. The teams were made up of people within the congregation, but not leadership; they worked very hard because they were invited to imagine God's future and came to believe that the Spirit of God was among them. Formation of these teams takes seriously the conviction that a congregation has the spiritual resources to discern what God is up to among them.

Cultivating Fresh Ways of Engaging Scripture

A missional culture is cultivated within a congregation as it learns to indwell and engage Scripture in new ways. For too long, congregations have been schooled in viewing Scripture as a tool to be used for a variety of reasons and to meet innumerable needs. Sometimes it's a help desk for finding an answer to a pressing problem. At other times it is used as a hammer to drive home a doctrinal position. Scripture has become like a bank safety deposit box holding a depository of information and knowledge that can be collected when needed. But all the uses of the Scripture as a tool fail to engage it as the narrative presence of God, who invites us into a story that reads and shapes us.

The missional leader cultivates an environment for indwelling the Scriptural narrative and inviting the congregation to join in that journey. Chris, the senior pastor of a university-based congregation on the West Coast, searched out the resources of Catholic and Protestant contemplative life to discover how to indwell the Scriptures rather than use the text as a tool to teach some principle or apply to some generic point about living. He then invited his leadership (staff and lay) to join with him in this process of living in and with a single piece of Scripture over an extended period of time. At first restive with this process of living with a text, these leaders discovered a new way of listening to God and one another. The result was a changed leadership environment for discerning their role in the congregation.

Cultivating New Practices, Habits, and Norms

Formation of a missional mind-set is not primarily a matter of technique and program. It is formation of a people in the habits and practices of Christian life. Our work with congregations shows there is a hunger among people to discover the habits and practices of Christian formation—what some, such as Richard Foster, call the celebration of the disciplines. But our work with pastors shows they have never been formed in these disciplines and practices; nor do the majority of them have consistent practices or habits that shape them as leaders (for example, indwelling Scripture as a listening process using Lectio Divina; most leaders use Scripture principally as a tool they master in the process of sermon preparation or teaching Bible studies). Other examples of such practices are regular fasting, silent retreat, and hospitality to strangers. Cultivating missional community requires recovery of such practices. It is not a quick fix; the processes always take longer than anticipated. There will be conflict, and our experience is that it is those leaders whose lives are formed by such practices who have the capacity to sustain themselves in this long and arduous journey.

Summary

The process of cultivating the missional congregation and leader is not linear. It is iterative, looping back and forth in an interplay within which one builds on the other. The next chapter presents a model for understanding the dynamics that have shaped the formation and identity of congregations and leaders for most of the twentieth century in North America. It lays the ground for introducing the change model used in this book to cultivate a missional environment.

CHAPTER 3

Change and Transition: Navigating the Challenges

"CAN THIS KIND OF TRANSFORMATION HAPPEN IN the church?"

The call was similar to a lot of others we've taken: a denominational executive facing budget cuts and staff reductions was trying to figure out how to help the system come to terms with a radically different world from the one in which it had grown and thrived. A pattern of financial decline had reached the tipping point; budget and program reductions were at the limit, and he knew they weren't getting at the need for more fundamental change. How could they address their challenges?

Bill is the senior pastor of a large, mainline congregation on the edge of a thriving metropolis in the Southeast. Lots of people are moving out to his area for the new exurbs and the promising big churches. Bill is aware; he knows it's fairly simple to market religious choices to these new customers. Yet for him and many on his board, it all seems somehow shallow in terms of what the Gospel is meant to be about. Bill calls us with questions similar to those of the denominational executive who was struggling with cutbacks. How do you engage this rapidly changing context missionally? How do you address the pressures staff are facing from a strong leader demanding answers and actions? What do you do when members start asking why they can't be like that big church across town that is booming with people? How is a congregation transformed into a missional community amid confusion and the challenges of rapid, discontinuous change?

Tim, a former parachurch leader who is now the young-adult-ministry pastor of a large suburban congregation on the West Coast, asks Alan if there is a conference he should attend that would help him in his new position. Al mentions a YS/Emergent conference in San Diego. Later, during the conference, Alan gets a bemused, excited call from Tim on his cell phone. "Al, I get it!" he chortles. "I'm sitting here in this conference and suddenly the lights have gone on: it's about Jesus and the kingdom, not programs, church, and individual souls!" It was a conversion moment for Tim.

Six months later he and Alan are sitting outside a coffee shop in the warm late summer sun as Tim describes the worship patterns he's introduced to express Kingdom values among young adults. Tim recognizes that most people in the congregation don't get what's happening. For most he's creating an interesting diversion they'll support as young adults head toward "real" church. "They don't get it!" Tim declares. "They don't understand it's about forming a radically different world!" Then he asks, "Can this kind of transformation happen in the church? It has to, but can it?"

He admits that the challenge is huge. The leadership summits led by big-name, megachurch leaders that his senior pastor has attended present an incredibly beguiling show of success. The senior pastor believes that the church needs a new plan to catch the next change cycle, and he wants youth ministry to line up behind the plan. Tim now knows that these big plans and programs are a million miles from the reality of the young adults he works with. He tells Alan that when he talks with the pastor about forming missional congregations of the Kingdom the senior pastor listens, agrees, and then passes it all through his default imagination of big programs, numerical growth, and a CEO mentality. Tim wants the missional life he is cultivating to happen within that congregation, but the leadership framework of the senior pastor ends the experiment after some eighteen months. He realizes the lesson he has to learn: one must understand something of a congregation's organizational culture before it is possible to cultivate missional imagination.

Congregations Can Change

A congregation can be transformed into a missional community. It doesn't need to be stuck in a cycle of growth, plateau, and decline. There are ways to innovate a new missional identity that is more than just an old pattern dressed in new words, but it requires some awareness and understanding of what is happening in congregations.

As we have emphasized in the first two chapters, God is present in churches today. Talking about the death of the church is just bad theology, sociology, and biblical imagination. Across the world, the church is moving through incredible transformation and growth despite terrible hardship. The majority of the church is no longer in Europe and North America; it's in the southern hemisphere. In sub-Saharan Africa, where AIDS and drought abound, Christian life and witness are vibrant. With few resources, the church is growing and vital; it is addressing the dire needs of its peoples in the places globalization and economic development have ignored or left behind. This is happening in Africa, a continent many Western leaders and corporations have written off as hopeless or of no economic value. In China the church is thriving for millions of men and women among whom God is present. By any standards, in Russia and Latin America the church is alive among thousands of poor men, women, and children who live out their common witness to the power of Jesus in the world. All of this is the work of God filling out the meaning of 1 Corinthians 1:25–28.

Yet the church in North America, Western Europe, and Australia is in serious decline. In these parts of the world it operates in a context of confusion, anxiety, resistance, and loss. Churches in these parts of the world are driven to recapture a lost sense of place and importance in their culture. They are beguiled by an ideology of growth, numbers, and trends. Energy is focused on marketing themselves as providers of religious goods and services to *seekers.* Yet despite the effort, a great many congregations and denominations continue to lose members. In one judicatory in the western United States, Alan was told that 70 percent of the congregations had plateaued over the past five years, with no new membership; the majority of them were shrinking. In response to the fear and anxiety provoked by this trend, leaders turn to programs and methodologies that promise recovery and growth through marketing and measuring. Some leaders confess they don't know what to do. They have little idea of the dynamics that get congregations and denominations into this kind of trouble in the first place.

An initial step in cultivating a missional community is understanding the dynamics that brought declining communities to their present crisis. This chapter presents a way of understanding this process.

A Map: *The* Three Zone Model *of* Missional Leadership

Figure 3.1 illustrates the three zones of organizational culture that congregations and denominations form at various times. Through much of the twentieth century, congregations thrived in a relatively stable and predictable context where churchgoing was the accepted norm. Denominations did well as a source of identity for people. New congregations were being built in expanding suburbs across the continent. Within this environment, a congregation would form its organization culture, beliefs, habits, and values. These cultures became the assumed norms by which congregations measured themselves. Throughout the century denominations, training schools, credentialing processes, leadership models, and organizational structures invested heavily in producing leaders with a highly developed capacity to perform the requirements and expectations of a church in this stable, predictable environment. The result is multiple generations of leaders with little experience or knowledge of how to lead when the context tips out of stability into discontinuous change. We are now in such a time. The Three Zone Model constitutes a framework to:

- Assist leaders in understanding the adaptive shifts in leadership style required amid such change
- Identify the skills and competencies required in each zone
- Help congregations understand their own location in massive change

The model describes an *emergent zone,* a *performative zone,* and a *reactive zone.* Every culture forms its own leadership imagination and habits, skills, and capacities. Each zone has two sections, upper and lower, with its own characteristics and associated leadership requirements.

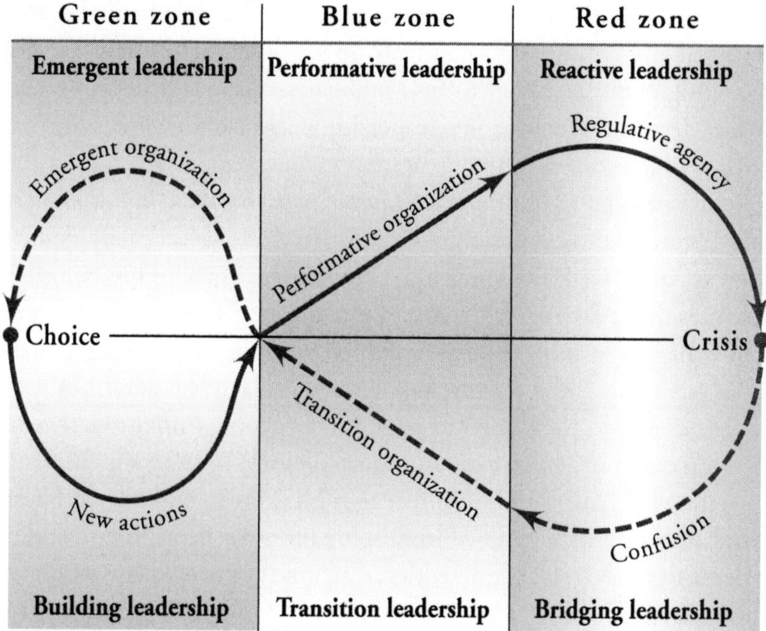

Figure 3.1. Three Zone Model of Missional Leadership.[1]

The Emergent Zone Congregation

In the emergent zone, a congregation's culture is one of maximum innovation and creativity in relationship to its context. An emergent congregation, like the color green, is characterized by creativity, energy, and the birthing of new forms of mission and ministry as it enters, listens to, and engages the community in which its people are located.

EMERGENT UPPER SECTION: PIONEERING. A congregation in this zone experiments and discovers various creative ways to indwell and engage the communities and neighborhoods in which its people are located. It is emergent in the sense that it's experimenting and discovering fresh ways of being God's missionary people. *Emergent* communicates the sense that when it comes to innovating missional life, this is a period of maximum experimentation in engaging their community. In this zone, a local church is adaptive; members are encouraged to cultivate experiments and interact with one another rather than wait on top-down, preplanned strategy. Clusters of people (who individually are unable to address how to be God's witnesses in a changing context) gather to find innovative ways of becoming missional. In the emergent zone, leadership cultivates the environments within which this missional imagination emerges.

In *Emergence: The Connected Lives of Ants, Brains, Cities, and Software,* Steven Johnson describes how ants—without leaders or explicit laws so far as we know—organize themselves into highly complex colonies that adapt to the environment as a single entity, altering size and behavior to suit conditions, exhibiting collective intelligence or what has come to be called emergence. Similarly, he describes how cities develop in the same way as ordinary people gather together to develop commercial, artistic, and social life; what emerges is the form of cities we identify as London, Paris, New York, and so on. These cities aren't so much planned from some central schema but gradually emerge from the multiple activities of all kinds of people. He describes this collective intelligence and creativity in a blunt, inelegant manner: "What features do all these systems share? . . . They get their smarts from below. . . . They are complex adaptive systems that display emergent behavior. . . . The movement from low-level rules to higher-level sophistication is what we call emergence."[2]

Richard Pascale, Mark Millemann, and Linda Gioja, authors of *Surfing the Edge of Chaos,* describe emergence this way: "Self-organization and emergence are two sides of the same coin of life. Self-organization is the tendency of certain (but not all) systems operating far from equilibrium to shift to a new state when their constituent elements generate unlikely conditions. . . . Interactions assemble themselves into a new order. . . . Simple patterns networked together undergo a metamorphosis. . . . *Emergence* is the outcome of all this: a new state or condition. . . . A jazz ensemble creates a new sound that no one could imagine from listening to the individual instruments."[3]

Missional leadership cultivates an environment in which the people of God imagine together a new future rather than one already determined by a leader.

The pioneering emergent zone is a period of maximum creativity and experimentation for a congregation. Members discover how to engage and imagine the shape of their life in relationship to the ceaselessly changing environment in which the congregation is located. They realize they can't predict or control outcomes, but there are factors that help to shape direction. Engagement with Scripture plays a big part, as does how they engage their context as well as their beliefs about what God is up to in the context. The actual forms of life and witness that emerge can't be predetermined. In the pioneering emergent zone, members learn as they go because they're in a situation where they've never been before. Leaders in this zone cultivate the creative energy and imagination of people through ongoing interaction between the indwelling of the biblical narrative and their experiences in the cultural context.

In one congregation, a group of people met for more than three months learning together how to dwell in Scripture. They spent the whole time reading the same passage (Luke 10: 1–12) and then listening to one another in terms of where they saw God at work in the passage and where the Gospel connected with their lives in terms of neighborhood and community. Much emerged from this process of spiritual discernment and listening to one another speaking their sense of God's calling. One woman heard God calling her from a job as a school teacher into work with the local hospice and caring for the dying. Another couple heard God calling them to a new sense of presence in their multiracial and changing neighborhood. They began walking regularly through the neighborhood, greeting people on the street and cleaning up the garbage left there. As they did this over several months, new conversations emerged as the couple connected with people in ways they would never have imagined. Confident missional leaders learn to trust that action and direction emerge out of the life and interaction of the community itself.

EMERGENT LOWER SECTION: EXPERIMENTING. A congregation gradually moves out of this phase of emergent creativity. The learn-as-you-go period wanes as appropriate habits and structures are built into the congregation. This shift represents the need to give form and order to what is emerging. The congregation's identity is still shaped by its interaction between Scripture dwelling and context. The congregational culture retains the ability to adapt through experimentation. Leadership capacities now involve developing structures, habits, and practices to allow the congregation to regularize its engagements with its context. The challenge in this zone is maintaining the tension between an active emergent culture that still percolates ideas and interacts dynamically with its environment and the need to embed habits and practices internally.

SOME CHARACTERISTICS OF EMERGENT ZONE LEADERSHIP. Leadership is comfortable with the ambiguity of loose coalitions drawn by pursuit of an elusive dream that seems out of reach. They manage ambiguity and don't need the quick closure of a solution or a large plan.

Leadership focuses a sense of shared conviction. We're together for something important; it has taken hold of us; we must pursue it. A vision is beginning to form the imagination but as yet it is still unclear because people are learning to understand and adapt to the changing environment. One group began a church plant in a downtown community in a large city. They learned how to enter, indwell, engage, and listen to the people of the local community. Mission and ministry emerged. As the plant grew, the founding team discovered others interested in developing similar plants in other communities. They were learning that rather than setting up independent local churches they would develop a single church with multiple congregations rooted in local neighborhoods. This vision was not seen in the beginning but emerged from their discovery of how to do local mission while at the same time sharing resources and leadership across the city.

This leadership cultivates a high level of social interaction in an environment where people are regularly involved in one another's lives. They have to be together to think out loud and test new ideas because they haven't been in this situation or environment before; they don't know what the next steps involve and need each other to figure out what to do. Communication is face-to-face; they confront challenges that can't wait for a scheduled committee meeting.

Emergent leadership works well in informal organizational life, at the beginning. There's no handbook, no set of rules. People come together to do what needs to be done at the moment; handbooks are written after the fact and on the go. Mission and vision statements are put together along the way, not at the beginning. Although there's a clear sense of being God's people in this particular context, the shape of it all can't be known at the outset; nor can something like a mission statement be done well initially.

People learn through a never-ending process of trial, error, and experimenting. Leaders create an environment where failure is permitted because they know it will happen often. It's more important to create a culture that values and permits risk.

This leadership keeps the congregation free of hierarchy and top-down or expert authority.

It excels in a situation or environment that is ambiguous, where groups face multiple challenges with no clear answers.

It focuses on the cultural rather than organizational formation of the community.

It sees challenge not as a crisis or exception to be managed but as an opportunity to be embraced.

Lastly, emergent leadership sees strategy as emergent, not linear. Leaders don't move according to a predetermined plan but learn to cultivate engagement and experiments that release the missional imagination of the people.

The Performative Zone Congregation

A congregational culture in the performative zone has the organizational structures, skills, and capacities required to perform well in a stable environment such as the middle decades of the twentieth century. The upper and lower sections of this zone function distinctly; we examine the upper performative zone and then move on to the reactive zone before returning to the lower performative zone. With reference to the model, this order follows the normal processes of change in any organization, moving predictably from the emergent period of creativity and adaptation into a period where it is attuned to the challenges of the environment. The organization now focuses on developing the skills and capacities that made it successful. Emphasis is no longer on developing adaptive skills but transferring learned skills to a new generation of leaders. This is why it is called a performative leadership zone.

PERFORMATIVE UPPER ZONE. The organizational culture focuses on performing well what has been learned and proven to work. The primary values are not innovation but skilled performance of a regular pattern of habits and actions. A performative zone congregation grows not through connecting with the people in its context but through people switching from other congregations. A good performative culture is creative; it thrives but increasingly lives off capital that was built in the emergent zone. Performative congregations and leaders have been the dominant form of organizational culture for North American churches throughout the twentieth century.

The performative congregation might be symbolized by the color blue, which implies solid, predictable performance resulting in success over the long haul. IBM uses blue to communicate dependable success; many banks use it to convey the same values. These cultures have been around for a long time; they are meant to be trusted to continue over the long run with the same principles and values. They're predictable; they function within clearly understood and accepted frameworks. But note an important characteristic about this organizational culture: a performative culture functions best in a stable, predictable environment; it is not organized to deal with discontinuous change. Performative organizations require this kind of environment to thrive. People attracted to them want stability rather than change. They deploy tactics, programs, and techniques that improve but do not fundamentally change their performance (better worship, preaching, evangelism, small-group life, disciple making process, mission trips, and so on). They resist change that requires them to shift significantly away from the habits, skills, and capacities that have brought success up to this point.

The performative zone was the cultural environment of the North American church for much of the twentieth century and still remains a primary factor for most growing congregations. The reason is straightforward. Until the last several decades of the century, the context of church life and leadership was one of relative continuity, predictability, and stability. Since the issues of radical and discontinuous change are very recent, almost all the habits, experience, and default positions of the church and its leadership are performative. In this context, churches and the denominational systems that served them could expect steady, if unspectacular, growth so long as they just performed in an average manner, stayed away from internal conflict, and kept programs updated. They functioned in an unusually long period of relative societal stability in North America. Needless to say, it has ended. In the last couple of decades, the wider culture has been radically destabilized. The result is congregations and leaders being ill prepared for the new environment.

SOME CHARACTERISTICS OF PERFORMATIVE UPPER ZONE LEADERSHIP AND ORGANIZATION. First, organizational culture is characterized by well-developed structure with clear lines of function, roles, and expectations, rather than a loose network of teams and groups as in the emergent zone. Leaders are professionals with a degree certified by a denomination to do the performative work of the church.

Second, large-scale planning displaces "just-in-time" emergent zone action. Planning, organization, and development flow outward from the center to the periphery. Leaders believe their job is to come up with plans and solutions for the congregation. They believe top-down planning brings the best results.

Third, specialization of roles and programs is the norm. Professional and credentialed leaders with specialized training and skills staff and lead the congregation. The laity is perceived as not having requisite training or skills.

Fourth, for leadership the focus is on ability to perform the skills required for running a congregation. Leadership is defined by set roles; leaders are chosen on the basis of ability to perform these roles.

Fifth, organizational hierarchy displaces loose association. Leaders move up or down in the congregation according to set processes. A constitution or operations manual is likely to define and regulate appropriate roles and functions in the system.

Sixth, the source of knowledge has shifted. Instead of a learning community, experts, professionals, and positional power send a message of knowing what to do and controlling what is done.

Seventh, most in the congregation experience a loss of overall, shared vision. Although a few people can articulate the vision that formed the congregation, in the performative zone people focus on current programs and how their needs are being met.

Eighth, formal groups, committees, and meetings replace a high level of informal social interaction. Communication has undergone a profound transformation. It is now formalized, taking place mostly through newsletters and information pieces, from the top down to the people. It is no longer a matter of just-in-time information about tasks to be accomplished; here is one-way information shared mmittees and staff members who want people to be involved in specific programs and events. Leaders believe that sharing information in the form of bulletins, newsletters, or Sunday announcements is communication.

Ninth, planning is rationalized, not emergent. It is based on the predictability of past results and an assumption that the future will continue to develop in much the same way as things have been in the past. As a result, planning continues the present culture into the future, moving from the center to the periphery, in a process in which people agree or disagree by means of vote or financial support.

DETOURED TO THE REACTIVE ZONE. Before describing the lower section of the performative zone, it is necessary to describe the reactive zone. The environment in which the congregation has functioned so well begins to change. For example, the congregation Alan pastored in downtown Toronto grew and flourished in a largely white, British emigrant community until the mid-1950s. At that point, new immigrant groups entered the community and younger Anglo couples moved to the new suburbs; the congregation continued to function with all its regular performative skills and programs. Over a period of several decades, the congregation dwindled to a few seniors who saw themselves as surviving in a community full of strangers. Their environment had changed radically. The congregation reacted to this change by closing out the new groups and working harder at doing what they had always found successful. They entered a spiral of decline and loss. When this happened, the congregation entered the reactive zone.

The Reactive Zone Congregation

The reactive zone describes what happens to an upper performative zone congregational culture when it encounters discontinuous change. As the cultural and social context goes through massive change, the skills and habits of a leader in an upper performative zone culture are insufficient to navigate in the new environment. The result is an experience of diffuse confusion, conflict, and anxiety in the face of unrelenting episodes of crisis without end. This is what happened in the Toronto congregation Alan entered in the early 1980s.

In another situation, a large congregation in Cincinnati experienced a period of major growth in the 1970s and 1980s, when it was the center of training and preaching for much of the evangelical population of the city. People drove in from all over the region to attend this flagship church. It had a great reputation, engaged in many creative experiments, and shaped the lives of several generations of leaders. But the times changed; other churches now took its place in an environment of seekers and megachurches. The community of the church shifted and the congregation gradually became an ethnic island in the neighborhood. By the end of the 1990s the congregation was in decline, most of the younger members had left for other, newer congregations, and the church's leadership was confused about the situation. A split ensued as a large number of people left to start another church, and there was ongoing concern about the inability of pastoral staff to lead the congregation.

In the reactive zone, leaders work harder, for longer hours, and with fewer resources at what they have been doing all along. They find they must address ever more crises with little time to imagine alternatives. But the answer is not trying harder and working longer. As the financial base of the systems erodes, with resultant cutbacks in personnel and budgets, more pressure is placed on fewer people. Productivity declines, creativity disappears, and stress grows. As the congregation or denomination moves deeper into crisis, leaders face demands to put out fires, manage dysfunction, and furnish solutions. These demands leave them with neither time nor energy to do the job for which they were hired. Feeling they have no answers, the leaders struggle or leave a situation they never signed on for. This is the reactive zone. Like the emergent zone and the performative zone, it has two distinct sections.

REACTIVE UPPER ZONE. Organizations and leaders in the upper section of the reactive zone respond to the changing environment by working harder to make their dominant habits, programs, and actions effective. A good example is the shift in technology that changed how newspapers set articles into print. In the mid-1970s, newspapers discovered they could quickly and efficiently type on a computer, which electronically sent articles to the press, bypassing the need for a typesetter. We take this process for granted now, but thirty years ago typesetters were a prevalent skilled profession that had existed for hundreds of years. Typesetting was a normative, performative activity of publishing. Until the revolutionary and profoundly disruptive change brought on by computerization, typesetting was an established performative zone culture that its practitioners thought would go on forever. Computers, in a very brief time, overturned a cultural artifact that had begun with Gutenberg and overturned (among many other things) a vocational way of life.

Typesetters responded to this change in a way that is typical of the upper reactive zone. They became reactive, seeking to create contractual agreements that would not simply maintain their position but turn back the clock and reestablish the domain they had enjoyed for hundreds of years (after all, they were the "blue-bloods" with hundreds of years of craft and influence). They staged strikes that closed down newspapers for long periods of time. For a while, the collective bargaining process guaranteed typesetters their job, with all the associated privileges. But this solution could last only for a brief time. The pace of technological change was too rapid. Soon newspapers simply didn't need typesetters at all. In less than a decade, they were obsolete and extinct. Yet nobody saw it coming! When an established, stable performative zone organization suddenly finds itself in the reactive zone (for those in the organization, it always feels as though change is sudden and unexpected), its leaders react by seeking to return to performative zone stability.

Churches that find themselves in the upper reactive zone respond in much the same way. We know of one denomination in which the majority of pastors were, by the early nineties, training in seminaries outside the denomination. Their denominational seminary has a performative culture, and students voted with their feet to be equipped elsewhere. As the seminary experienced a critical loss of students, its principal and board (along with the denominational leadership) feared loss of the cultural ethos that gave them both privilege and control. They responded in a typical reactive zone manner by developing regulations that required all candidates for ministry in their denomination to attend their seminary. The assumption was that this would return the school and denomination to its previous dominance and reassert its cultural values. The official reason they gave was the need to ensure that candidates were trained in the denomination's polity and culture, but the underlying motive lay in their drive to reduce their own anxiety and rescue the denomination. As is typical of reactive zone leaders, they responded by trying to regulate.

Blue zone organizations (Figure 3.1) operate out of performative skills, values, and assumptions and reward those best at performing within this culture. Men and women ascend the leadership ladder by being good performative leaders. They experience the reactive zone as a place of confusion where the status, regulations, rules, and resources of success no longer seem to function, so they react by reasserting performative zone values and skills in an attempt to wrestle the organization back to stability. For example, in one denomination a large number of its congregations were losing faith in its ability to address a crisis of declining membership and financial loss; the executive initiated a capital campaign to pay down debt and repair buildings (performative solutions to discontinuous change). The majority of congregations passively refused to support the campaign. In response, the executive constructed a letter—which wiser heads advised him not to send—stating that in the future congregations failing to participate would be refused grant loans and loan guarantees for any building projects. The reactive zone is about using regulation to gain back control of an organization. It is the equivalent of biblical Israel demanding it be allowed to return from the frightening desert to slavery in Egypt.

Like the gathering strength of a hurricane, the forces that create a reactive zone situation take time to develop. But because they develop out of the sight of those within the congregation and denomination, they are not expected and therefore not seen. The reactive zone seems to emerge suddenly and without warning, undermining the viability of church life. Because they do not understand the situation, leaders default to the performative zone, with skills that have always worked up to this point. They try to return the congregation to the performative zone in which they were successful and excelled. That route may bring short-term anxiety reduction, but it is not an option for moving into the future. The power of past habit nevertheless continues to determine response in the reactive zone.

REACTIVE ZONE: CRISIS. For some time, leaders continue to function as if past habits will work because it's the only way they know how to respond and there's little capacity to read what is actually happening. Sooner or later, however, comes growing awareness that regulatory, performative reaction is making no difference in a deteriorating situation.

Members of a midlevel judicatory found themselves in a reactive zone crisis. The executive and board described what they called positive, proactive steps taken several years earlier to address a financial crisis. These steps were classic performative zone responses:

1. They implemented denominational regulations that required each congregation to increase its per capita giving.
2. They amalgamated several marginal congregations and sold their excess property to pay down the judicatory's debt.
3. They covered a growing yearly deficit from legacy funds.

Three and a half years later, the financial crisis returned. Their performative action failed to address the deeper issue of the need to transform the judicatory's organizational culture in a period of rapid discontinuity.

This example illustrates the nature of the crisis in the reactive zone. In response, an organization makes program cuts and staff reductions as the funding base erodes. Denominational systems are no longer able to function within financial arrangements developed for a twentieth-century world. The reactive zone crisis manifests in a variety of ways:

- People become anxious, expressing anger at leaders for their inability to address the situation.
- Staff retreat into ever-deeper silos to protect their dwindling budget and positions. Subtle power and political struggle emerges as they fight over policy, staff, and finances in order to maintain control.
- Battle lines form around issues other than those that are critical to the life of the system. People take sides and demonize

each other over secondary issues, which further reduces the system's ability to address the real crisis.

- A constitution, books of order, and operations manuals are used to assert control.
- Some opt out (emotionally or physically) of the organization's life. They might do so by setting up their own network or suborganization. The system becomes Balkanized around secondary issues that deepen the crisis.
- As pressure increases, leaders resign to relieve stress in their lives.

REACTIVE LOWER ZONE: THE CONFUSED CONGREGATION. The lower section of the reactive zone marks a period of maximum confusion and discouragement. One executive responsible for more than 180 congregations described how she had worked hard as a pastor to bring transformation to her congregation. She enjoyed some success in adding a significant number of people to the church rolls but recognized this was not the missional transformation needed. She knew how to increase membership, organize efficiency, and plan programs but not how to cultivate the missional life she believed was essential.

Because of her success as a pastor, she was invited into an executive position in the judicatory. Five years into the job, she was discouraged and confused. Her days were occupied with congregational and pastoral crises. She was worn out from dealing with a fractious church culture in which she was barely treading water as she struggled to keep up with crisis after crisis. More than anything else, she was confused and no longer knew what to do. Something more basic than new programs was required, but she'd exhausted her energy on proliferating demands and lost hope that there was a way to address the crisis of leadership. Her words, spoken quietly when the other executives weren't in the room, were painful: "When I finish with this job in a few years, I don't think I'll ever go back to a church again."

This leader was caught in the reactive zone, without understanding the nature of the shift from performative zone to reactive zone leadership. Many leaders find themselves in the in-between situation illustrated by Figure 3.2.

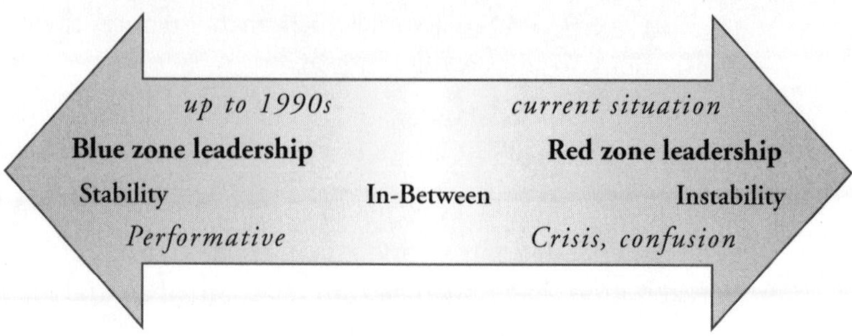

Figure 3.2. The Move from the Performative Zone to the Reactive Zone.

There are two leadership challenges in the reactive zone. First, one must become aware that the challenges are no longer routine and can't be addressed by the methods and assumptions of the performative zone. Simply put, the system is in a situation where performative strategies, values, and approaches will never work. Decisions must be made and action taken that no longer fit an established paradigm. The issues the organization faces are not well understood, and attention needs to be given to developing people's awareness and understanding of the situation, not to strategic plans or organizational change.

Second, the reactive zone is a place of instability and crisis that must be managed, not fixed. While people are experiencing crisis, they cannot risk substantive change. The organization needs a measure of stability to cultivate the creativity and innovation required to rediscover missional life. As is discussed in the next chapter, the primary skills for doing this involve cultivating dialogue and listening across the system or denomination. This is usually not the first instinct of reactive zone leaders in crisis, who often address their own anxiety by coming up with some form of bold plan (we think of BHAG, or "big, hairy, audacious goals"). The theory behind this approach is to find some new vision or focal mission before the system enters crisis. This supposedly bold new vision (a version of what the TV series "Star Trek" used to designate as "where none have gone before") might involve reaching a certain group or type in the community, or planting a huge number of new congregations over a ten-year period, and so on.

The vision is supposed to galvanize the membership and turn the ship around. As we will see, it actually stops the process of listening to and engaging people who are in crisis. As a methodology it is leader-driven, from the top, and does not engage the people themselves in forming a new imagination. In most cases, the bold new future soon begins to look a whole lot like the same old present, and the main result is that leaders spend down hope among the people.

A reactive zone crisis is a transition where people recognize the impossibility of regaining a lost past but have not yet internalized how to become another kind of culture. In this zone, the organizational culture is fragile. People are tentative and suspicious; they grieve the loss of their world and the awareness that it will not return.

In the reactive zone, the role of the leader is not to escape the crisis through a BHAG but invite people into a place of dialogue and engagement amid crisis. It is there that people (God's people among whom the Spirit is present) begin to discern and imagine a different future for themselves. This leadership calls for a combination of performative and learning organization skills.

Transition Organizations: The Performative Lower Zone

Once a congregation in the reactive zone realizes its regulatory responses are no longer working and the crisis reaches a critical level, the congregation faces a number of options. It might continue in a state of distress and move into a period of steep decline leading to death; it might seek out a leader who will impart a new vision and remake the congregation in a radically new mold; it can choose to enter the performative lower zone, which has the potential of inviting people to learn again how they might imagine fresh ways of being God's people. This is a place of choice, one which is difficult because the work of moving through the performative zone is hard. At this point in its life, the congregation is caught in a significant polarity. On one side are the voices and forces demanding radical action and bold innovation. This usually comes in the form of a demand for significant shift in direction, perhaps involving wholesale change of leadership and seeking out a leader who can furnish a vision and manage a new direction. On the other side are those who want to maintain elements of the tradition and story that have shaped the congregation and its past. This is a significant tension, and the temptation is to resolve it in a win-lose direction whereby one side comes to shape the agenda. But what the move into the lower section of the performative zone does is not close down the polarity, but instead invites both sides to engage one another. This is about leadership that manages the polarity rather than solving it by adopting one side or the other. It is in the tension of managing the polarity that the potential for creativity and new life can begin to emerge from among people themselves. But this is not an inevitable or evolutionary process; the congregation and its leaders must consciously choose this direction.

Now is the appropriate time to return to our discussion of the performative zone. A congregation in transition finds itself in a radically different organizational culture and a wholly new kind of world, but it is still shaped by the memory and habits of its successful performative culture.

In the transitional lower performative zone, the congregation is in an environment in which it begins to learn and discover new ways of being God's people. This is the place where habits and capacities begin to be shaped, but it is also a fragile period requiring wise leadership. In the lower performative zone, emphasis is not on seeking to create a BHAG but on cultivating an environment of listening and dialogue among people. The leader in this part of the performative zone understands that top-down solutions don't bring cultural change. What is required is a process that cultivates new imagination among people themselves.

In this zone, the leader needs to work with the symbols, experiences, and narratives that appropriately communicate the reality of God's story. These symbols (Word, Sacrament, worship) represent both the stability and the instability that God brings about among a people. But the lower performative zone represents a kind of stability different from that of the upper section, which had to do with confidence in things continuing as they always have been and the conviction that the future will be more or less like the past. In the lower section of the performative zone, this kind of stability is gone. The experience here is more like everything being out of control, so to move toward an emergent zone environment people must first experience some stability. This requires practices and habits of Christian life and regularization of structures and order. This lower performative zone cultivates stability as a prelude to creativity and risk. A primary way in which this stability is afforded is in identifying some of the key elements of the congregation's culture that should be strengthened and emphasized as innovation is introduced. For example, this is when worship needs to be shaped and led with excellence; preaching, visitation, and a number of other elements experienced as deeply embedded in the congregation's life must be done with a high level of skill and care. By performing these elements well, one reintroduces a level of confidence and stability while innovative experimenting is developing.

This lower part of the performative zone requires transitional leadership. At this point, the congregation is not yet ready to engage in the creative behaviors described in the emergent zone. People don't know how to go about this kind of change; they're working through their issues of loss, confusion, and anger. They need time to understand what has happened, evaluate their current reality, and test new ways of being the church. People first have to be prepared. All of this takes time. Leaders must give attention to the important difference between change and transition.

As we discussed in Chapter Two, change is what happens to us from forces outside ourselves over which we have no control. Most of us deal fairly well with continuous change, which is ongoing, gradual, and expected. For most of the twentieth century developmental, continuous change went on within established, performative organizations that operated inside a cultural framework where things made sense and could be interpreted. Leaders developed a variety of skills and competencies to deal with constant change in a way that would return a state of normalcy and predictability. Over time people developed an expectation that whenever disruptive change occurred they should, could, and would return to normal.

But discontinuous change is much more disturbing and difficult. Unlike the continuous form, it creates a situation that requires something different from and more potent than the normal habits and skills that were so useful during a stable period of continuous change. Congregations do not do well with this unexpected, dramatic change; they need entirely different skills and capacities from those that have served them well in the past.

Besides continuous and discontinuous change, there is also transition, which is our inner response to change coming from outside ourselves. This inner response can be powerful. One morning Alan was sitting in a meeting in the eastern part of the United States when his cell phone went off. It was his brother calling to saying that their mother was in the hospital and wasn't going to live more than several days. That's discontinuous change by anyone's definition! As Alan went back into the meeting, he heard little of the discussion of church leadership that was going on around him. He couldn't remember what was said over the next hour. He was in transition, responding to the distressing news that he had just received.

Transition is a powerful reality in our lives. When a congregation loses members or is forced to make budget cuts, people respond along a spectrum of emotions. Some get angry at the leaders for failing to fix the situation. Others deny the situation by trying harder to make old programs work (recalling the well-known notion of madness as doing the same thing over and over again even though you know it doesn't work). One congregation in the Northeast experienced a precipitous loss of membership over a two-year period, from about 950 to just over 650. When teams of people began interviewing members about this situation, they saw a range of emotions, from grief to apathy; but the dominant one was a sense of inertia, anger, and loss of hope in anything changing. These are all illustrations of the deep, inner emotional response to discontinuous change called transition.

In a congregation struggling with discontinuous change, it isn't the changes that will defeat the leader but the transitions. As the congregation enters the crisis and confusion of discontinuous change, the reflexive response of leaders is to come up with a change plan to fix the crisis and return the organization to its normal experience of effectiveness and success. The problem with this response is that the plans focus on change; they ignore transition. Unless an organization learns to address its transition issues, it will never create an effective change process. The Missional Change Model, which we discuss in Chapter Five, explains how to lead through transition so as to address discontinuous change.

Summary: Principles *for* Leading Missional Transformation

Missional leadership requires the capacity to lead a congregation through the all the zones discussed in this chapter. Given our current environment, however, leaders need to cultivate an emergent zone culture within congregations. This takes time and requires skills not normally a part of a leader's training. The next section of the book presents a way of developing these skills and capacities. The Three Zone Model makes it clear that differing styles and capacities are required, depending on the location of the congregation.

We have introduced the Three Zone Model to hundreds of leaders. They connect with its framework as a tool for understanding the complexities of missional leadership. Some ask if it's necessary to cycle continuously through the zones. They wonder if it is possible to short-circuit the reactive zone. The short answer is that it isn't. Sooner or later, every congregation moves through the cycle in one form or another. This is about God's engagement with the church. There's always tension between a church missionally engaging its context and becoming colonized by its culture. Scripture presents a recurring story of God taking people into the desert, or into captivity, as a means of renewing and converting them all over again to faithful living. Reactive zone life will always play a part; there is no arriving.

It is useful to keep in mind five basic principles for leading missional transformation, as we go forward to discussion of leadership through a period of transition:

1. No performative zone performance organization lasts forever. Sooner or later the context changes to such a degree that the primary programs, resources, and skills that worked well in a long period of stability become a liability.
2. We can't see all the steps along the way. In the performative zone, change was predictable and manageable. Predetermined strategies defined desired outcomes. That world is over. Discontinuous change is the norm; we need new images and paradigms for leading where we can't predict outcomes.

3. Any performative or reactive zone congregation can adapt. The natural world offers examples of organisms that adapt to discontinuous change. Over thousands of years wheat, for example, adapted to changing ecological environments by developing new variants. The key to missional change is innovating an adaptive culture.
4. Adaptive change happens by cultivating emergent zone culture. This involves the ability to create multiple experiments around the edge and then connect them with one another to form a co-learning environment. It's a bottom-up rather than top-down process.
5. Cultivating a missional congregation requires new leadership skills and capacities.

Chapter Five introduces the Missional Change Model, a powerful way of understanding the processes required to cultivate the missional congregation. But first let's take a look at the big picture, the context in which a missional congregation lives and that shapes it dramatically.

CHAPTER 4

The Big Picture: Understanding the Context of the Missional Congregation

ENORMOUS CHANGES ACROSS OUR CULTURE REQUIRE fresh thinking about developing innovative experiments, habits, and attitudes among communities of God's people. This chapter explains the sources of the Missional Change Model within the context of these massive shifts in our culture. This material gives leaders the reasons underlying our recommended process of change. In Chapter Five we describe how the model works.

The Mission Change Model is based on (1) assumptions about the nature of change from our practical experience in innovating missional change in congregations and denominational systems, and (2) research conducted for more than forty years by anthropologists and sociologists looking at what happens on the ground when significant adaptive change is demanded.

The Whole *and* Its Parts

The Missional Change Model requires some understanding of systems, by which we mean any group of two or more interconnected and interdependent parts that interact and function as a whole. This interconnectedness makes the whole greater than the sum of its parts. In working together, these parts make systems complex and give them "personalities." For example, if you visit a local church over a period of time you will see that its personality is different from those of other churches. The church personality is partly the reason we are attracted to, or reactive to, various church communities.

Like organisms, organizations are made up of many interconnected parts, from a small number to tens of millions. They are systems functioning on various scales resulting in complex sets of behavior that need to be interpreted and understood at several levels.

In recent history, the Western imagination has developed ways of understanding reality through the processes of reduction, simplification, and analysis. This is the world of Newtonian mechanics in which reality was conceived as an infinite set of individual elements coming together and moving apart on the basis of invariable laws. We assumed that we could understand reality by (1) determining the specific laws, (2) breaking things down into their constituent parts for analysis, and (3) formulating actions built on these two processes. Although this understanding has value, it is a form of reductionism that ignores the many variables affecting all the interactions in a system.

The human brain is an example of a complex, adaptive system. The laws describing its functionality and behavior are qualitatively different from those that govern individual units, the neurons, synapses, and cells. It is impossible to describe or predict the rich, diverse behavior of the brain simply by extrapolating from the behavior of individual units. The study of a single neuron, or group of neurons, cannot describe the activity produced by the entire brain. The same is true for a congregation.

A congregation is made up of a series of relationships, traditions, and networks ceaselessly interacting and affecting one another. These are never just one-to-one relationships. They are always complex because of the many interactions and engagements happening at the same time. In this sense, a congregation as a system is not amenable to simplistic strategies that assume it is possible to predict and manage predefined outcomes by analyzing or naming its parts or aspects.

System Change *in* Congregations

Leaders must understand several principles of how congregations—as systems—can and do change. These principles frame the Missional Change Model and give it context.

Principle One: Focus on the Culture, Not the Organization

The culture of a congregation is how it views itself in relationship to the community, the values that shape how it does things, expectations of one another and of its leaders, unspoken codes about why it exists and whom it serves, how it reads Scripture, and how it forms a community. We have observed many attempts to change how congregations work in terms of their organization, programs, and specific ways of conducting core practices such as worship, teaching, and discipleship. Experience has taught us that programmatic and organizational change, though it has some short-term effect, does not result in the innovation of long-term missional change. We have learned that unless the culture of a congregation is changed all the sound programs and organizational changes that have been implemented evaporate. As a result, the congregation eventually reverts back to previous habits.

An example of this process is seen in the North American penchant for diets. We all have heard about the rising percentage of severely overweight North Americans and the obesity crisis that results in multiple diseases and high death rates. In response, people buy a huge number of diet books to help them lose weight. There is nothing wrong with the advice that many of these books offer, and the programs and regimens recommended are sound. Despite all the diet books and programs, obesity is not going away but is instead getting worse. Why? Because the books and their programs don't address the deeper cultural issues that make eating certain foods the norm, that shun exercise, and that encourage a sedentary lifestyle. Something deeper than diet books and programs is required to change the situation. A cultural transformation is needed.

Similarly, innovating missional congregations is not primarily a matter of programs or organizational change. It requires a profound change in congregational culture.

Principle Two: Focusing on Culture Does Not Change Culture

Searching for happiness cannot bring happiness; it is the result of things other than the search. This is true for culture change, which always derives from other factors and influences. Culture change happens in a congregation when God's people shift their attention to elements such as listening to Scripture; dialoguing with one another;

learning to listen; and becoming aware of and understanding what is happening in their neighborhood, community, and the places of their everyday lives. Instead of seeing these places and relationships as potential for church growth, they come to be seen as the places where God's Spirit is present and calling us to enter with listening love. This shift sees God at work in one's context and seeks to name what God might be up to. It is about seeing the church in, with, and among the people and places where we live, rather than in a specific building with a certain kind of people.

Principle Three: Change Takes Time and Small Steps

For many of us, cultivating a missional imagination seems like a lot of talk. We want a fast way to fix problems and develop solutions. But if we get caught up in the rush to resolve anxiety by moving quickly to solutions, we are likely to do more of what we've already been doing with the same outcomes. Missional transformation occurs in a series of small movements, actions, and behaviors among God's people.

Principle Four: Baby Steps

Small steps and short-term wins are the best approach, rather than big programs or large-scale planning.

Principle Five: Starting with "Alignment" Is Not the Answer

Some strategic planning processes preach about alignment, or lining up all the congregation's strategy, structure, staff, skills, systems, style, people, resources, and shared values around a common goal or vision. This is a classic upper Performative Zone practice. The only way to create alignment, however, is to negate the messy reality that God's future emerges from God's people nonlinearly and unpredictably. Alignment assumes it's possible to define outcomes from the front end. Such certainty is impossible in a context of discontinuous change. Alignment does not take place at the front end of a transformation; it emerges from experiments, dialogue, and engagements together in the work of the Emergent Zone.

The Cultural Context *for* Congregations

Cultivation of missional systems does not occur in a vacuum. Because all our questions about the mission of God's people are contextual, we must ask about the current social location of members of North American congregations. Specifically, we must ask what the social location is of those congregations and denominations of the formerly European-based Protestant churches that still form a major part of Christian life on this continent. What are the real experiences of the men and women in these congregations at this moment? The next sections attempt to answer these questions. Later sections address how the Missional Change Model engages the questions.

Massive Transitions *in* Public *and* Personal Life

It is not only the church that has been experiencing discontinuous change; our whole society is in massive transition. Congregations are populated with men and women who feel increasingly adrift in a context filled with both global and local challenges that no longer seem resolvable using the actions, beliefs, and practices that worked for them in the past. Since the end of the Cold War, society has encountered a growing number of fracture lines. Our lived experience is that no one knows how to address these fractures, and our learned ways of working out our place in the world no longer seem adequate. The result is confusion and anxiety.

Insecurity *and* Threat

German sociologist Ulrich Beck summarizes the reemergence of insecurity, even before a post–September 11 world, as people's primary experience. He says, "Studies show that more and more people consider their life and well-being under threat. . . ."[1] Even with a decline in violent crime, people feel more insecure; they view their external environment as a zone of danger, filled with threatening strangers. Communities are gated and schools become lock-down zones; once-normal socialization among children becomes bullying; parents see other children as the enemy or a threat. The sense of being together in a community is replaced by smaller and smaller group alliances that protect against any and all who appear different or threatening.

The disappearing middle-class sensibilities that were once the cornerstone of identity and security can no longer be taken for granted. Unemployment, Beck points out, "no longer threatens only marginal groups, but also the middle sections of society, even groups (such as doctors and executives) which, until a few years ago, were considered the very quintessence of middle-class economic security. Moreover, this is happening on such a massive scale that the difference between unemployment and threatening unemployment is becoming insignificant to the affected parties."[2]

This experience is not abstract to us. A friend of Alan's, a chemical engineer in his midforties, found himself without work for the second time in five years. The division he managed in an agricultural chemical firm was abruptly closed. He represents a middle class that, a few years ago, assumed that a professional degree and twenty years' experience meant security in terms of salary, work, and pension. No more! This man is a devout Catholic who wouldn't miss a Sunday Mass. It is a significant part of his life. When he attends Mass, his experience is not rooted in discussion about becoming a missional church; he's not concerned with whether or not his congregation is a chaplain to society or a consumer depot for religious goods and services. He focuses on the fact that he lives every day with an anxiety and confusion that has few places for expression. He seeks God, but not in terms of the theological frameworks of a cultural critique of modernity or the meaning of the kingdom of God for a missional church's engagement with the Gospel. We are not saying these concerns are unimportant, but they miss the point in terms of engaging the lived reality of most men and women in congregations today.

People are losing their orientation. The political, social, and economic systems that brought prosperity over the past fifty years no longer function and people see no alternatives. They feel caught in a web of change they neither understand nor control. The result is a high level of anxiety, insecurity, and confusion. At the same time, most people have no words to explain these experiences nor names for the forces shaping their lives and creating insecurity. This is because the stories that used to explain their experiences no longer seem relevant or applicable. Faced with unnamed and unseen forces controlling their lives—as illustrated by the plethora of TV programs and movies dealing with alien and unseen forces that threaten to plunge human life into the abyss of chaos—people feel anxious and paralyzed.

As Beck tells us, we live in a social context "in which everything that was conceived of as belonging together is being drawn apart"[3]; the accepted, normal story of twentieth-century middle-class life has been shattered and nothing but uncertainty appears to be taking its place. We are in a global-risk society where traditional means of forming life (family, church, nation, business, law, and politics) have been drained away, leaving a world that appears without direction.

Further Retreat *into the* Private Sphere

For Zygmunt Bauman, who teaches sociology at the Universities of Leeds in England, one result of uncertainty and massive change is that people turn inward to their private selves, and at the same time turn the public world into a means of achieving their own private security or identity. He responds to the question of where we find ourselves by investigating what has happened to public forms of communication in Western culture.

Bauman sees the public world (where we engage one another in questions of common meaning, purpose, and the good) as evaporating. The bridge between private and public has been dismantled to the point that "the sole grievances aired in public are sackfuls of private agonies and anxieties. . . ."[4] Communication has become largely narcissistic—private therapy through public discourse with gurus such as Dr. Phil and Oprah. Examples of this trend are seen in contemporary preaching, a public event that uses biblical narrative to help people make their lives work. The biblical narrative thus becomes a how-to tool to help people in their private, personal lives, a kind of chicken soup for the Christian life. The biblical narrative is colonized by narcissistic, private anxieties in the service of therapy.

Our society offers few opportunities to dialogue with one another about the larger realities we face together. There are increasingly fewer places where we can engage in a discourse that invites us to become aware of and give language to the forces shaping our lives. The type of preaching described here does not allow such an exchange. Instead, it offers people analgesics borrowed from the wider culture that are baptized with biblical texts. This preaching fails to cultivate an environment in which people can ask questions about the forces shaping their lives and fueling their anxiety and confusion. The image of Jesus calling Lazarus from the grave comes to mind; most preaching is about how to cope with a life wrapped in grave clothing that is never removed.

Bauman's work has serious implications for the challenge of forming missional systems:

> Now the definition of the public has been reversed. It has become a territory where private affairs and exclusive possessions are put on display. . . . The "public" has been emptied of its own separate contents; it has been left with no agenda of its own—it is now but an agglomeration of private troubles, worries, cravings and problems. It is patched together of the individual cravings for assistance in making sense of private, as yet inarticulate, emotions and states of mind, for instruction in how to talk about such emotions in a language which others would comprehend, and for advice about how to deal with the flow of experience which individuals find too difficult to cope with. The list of "public issues" is no different from that of "private affairs. . . ."[5]

We can see this phenomenon of making private need paramount in the increasing number of people who make it known that the forms of life in a particular congregation are no longer enough for them. As a result, they seek another congregation that will satisfy their needs. To them, it is vividly clear that the public gathering of the people of God has a single, primary purpose: meeting the private, personal needs of each individual member. Contemporary forms of public worship manifest the same dynamics. The vast majority of new songs sung repeatedly by the assembled crowd on a Sunday morning are about private, emotive experiences the individual wants to have with God in the midst of a crowd.

In such a privately focused world, people lose the capacity to communicate with one another out of a common, coherent language. Public settings become the location for expressing the inarticulate emotions and states of mind that now shape conversation. This is significant for understanding how the innovation of missional life must happen in a congregation. People no longer have the language with which to articulate the meaning of their experience of discontinuity and anxiety except in terms of the private and personal. This is why, in part, the public world becomes the arena of the private, bartering the promise of a solution to private anxiety. The public becomes a place where people receive private, therapeutic language with which to find common meaning for their lives. Hence, the popularity of television shows such as "Oprah" with their constant stream of self-help advice. These programs daily display people like us who live in the confusion and anxiety of our current context. They appear to find ways of dealing with these stresses, which become the vicarious means of addressing our own private angst.

The Importance *of* Narrative *for* Missional Congregations

The move to counter this broken social context and form a missional congregation begins with cultivating an environment that invites people to address their experience and to reconnect with the memory of the biblical narrative in a way that grounds their lives in a story bigger than their private needs. Missional leaders cultivate ways of engaging people in dialogue and discussion that brings to voice their experiences and locates them within God's narrative.

Missional change begins with the actual narratives, questions, issues, and anxieties of people at this moment. It connects these experiences to the biblical narrative that offers a language for understanding and making sense of those experiences. Language is not just about words, and narratives are not about a dead story or memory. Language is more than a game groups use to grasp power from others. Narrative shapes and forms reality; it reflects people's deepest convictions. Language and story are the atmosphere we humans need to live in because they shape us and change the reality of our world. For people to become something more than a collection of individuals crowding together for warmth, they must recover a common narrative that gives sense to the present and shapes their future. This is what has been lost, displaced by the conviction that only the present moment and only the individual self amid other selves can bear any meaning.

We are now a culture that lives off fragments of past stories glued together for a moment. We search for ways to buy new experiences and fresh moments that might connect us to something other than ourselves. This is why leaders need the ability to cultivate an environment where people can communicate with each other about the social context they experience and rediscover the lived memory of their larger narrative in Scripture.[6] The biblical story confronts; it challenges our constructions, deconstructs our world, and presents the possibility of inhabiting another way of life. The innovation of the missional congregation begins by inviting people into the discovery of this narrative.

In *After Virtue,* theologian Alasdair MacIntyre describes human beings as essentially storytelling animals. We cannot understand ourselves in society apart from the repertoire of stories that constitute our lives.[7] For MacIntyre "there is no way to give us an understanding of any society, including our own, except through the stock of stories which constitute its initial dramatic resources."[8] According to MacIntyre, we can recover a direction and purpose that are more than arbitrariness or construction of self, by understanding that human life is rooted in narrative and tradition. To be a human is to indwell a narrative.

A narrative has several characteristics. It comprises a story that is moving somewhere; it gives a social group a story that tells where it is going and what the group will look like when it arrives. There is purpose and quest within the narrative calling a group in a specific direction and toward a particular goal.

Narratives do not emerge *de novo* but are formed over time by communities and shaped into and by a tradition. The identity of the Jewish people, for example, is formed out of a series of stories within a tradition of four to five thousand years. Their identity is shaped by a specific story ("a wandering Aramaian was my father"). It is the story of God calling Abraham and forming his descendants into a peculiar people. The continuing story about exile and exodus rises out of the past, forms the Jewish identity, and is embedded in rituals such as Passover and Hanukkah that are repeated every year. Every Jew is born into this tradition and given this story from birth. Who they are and how they experience and read their world are framed and determined by the richness and depth of this narrative tradition.

MacIntyre compares narrative with the stage on which a play takes place. We are all born onto a stage in the sense that we enter a life that's already going on and a script is being acted out by parents, teachers, ministers, doctors, friends, officials, and others. In this sense we are born into a tradition. We enter a world with a particular narrative that has concrete life and meaning within a social group. As the postmodern scholar Jenny Rankin says, "Narrative is coming to be recognized as the ground in which the relations through which and the vehicle by which humans develop knowledge of themselves and the world they inhabit. [sic] It can now be seen that human agency, intentionality, actions, perceptions, and experiences are conceived, understood and mediated by cultural and personal narratives, and that the struggle for recognition is played out between humans in the narrative field."[9]

Because narrative creates and sustains social community, it's the glue, the atmosphere of all social life. The key to innovating missional community is formation of a people within a specific memory and narrative. This begins by engaging the lived stories of people and bringing those stories into dialogue with the biblical narratives. Missional leaders need skills and resources for creating an environment in a congregation that invites people into these dialogues. Our friend Chris Erdman in Fresno, California, has become a gifted leader in these areas. He has listened to the narratives of his people, especially among the leadership of the church. Some of those leaders initially resisted his leadership. They didn't really want all the talk and pushed for a strategic plan that would achieve results and give clear leadership within the congregation. But Chris persisted. He gathered people together, invited them to share their stories with each other, and asked them to bring those stories into contact with the Scriptures. Chris did not use Scripture to give people answers or a few new tactics based on its "principles." Rather, he gradually taught his leaders the skills of indwelling the Scripture, of listening to God in the midst of the Word. The process took time, but Chris did not give up. The leaders would attend retreats, which were not so much big planning events as a place to learn how to go more deeply into the processes of listening to Scripture. Out of this, they committed to some simple daily practices around prayer, Scripture, and discernment. What slowly emerged was a growing sense that among the people of this church there were wonderful, God-given dreams waiting to be called forth in the context of their neighborhood and community. There is now a real sense in this congregation that God is at work among them. Some of these dreams are being turned into action across the street from the church in a housing development, as well as among students at the state university.

Why Narrative Matters *in* Innovating *a* Missional Congregation

What are the implications of this perspective on the recovery of narrative for innovating missional congregations? One implication recognizes that we have been schooled in a narrative that believes meaning is already given objectively in the world. Our role is therefore to identify that meaning and then shape our systems around these objectively described realities of church life. Hence the focus on strategic planning. There are alternative narratives, however, that are closer to what God reveals in the biblical narratives. The Missional Church Model we discuss in more detail in Chapter Five is based on these other ways of understanding the nature of the world.

Another implication involves the nature of language itself. In its specificity to people and culture, language is about the unique way in which human beings give meaning to the world through the act of naming. As we name things, events, experiences, and relationships, we place them within a larger framework of meaning. In fact, we are creating and forming the world in which we live. This is what God is doing in speaking Creation into being. Language is the power given to Adam when he is invited to name the animals and birds. Adam (and by extension all human beings) is invited to co-create reality with God in the act of naming. Similarly, through its narrative the church becomes a co-creator with its Lord in an emergent future none can predict or predefine from this end of the story.

We use language all the time to create worlds. Children do it with each other. So much of their play is experimenting with words, with language, to create imaginary worlds populated with exotic creatures and beings. I've just read A. A. Milne's story of Christopher Robin and Winnie the Pooh to my grandson. These words or stories are not only about a world Milne created but also about a story I am creating with and for my grandson. Language and story form a world. Reading the great confessions and instituting the Eucharist by reading Scripture every week forms us in a way of life; it creates the social reality of the church. Some of the greatest literary artists do the very same thing with language to create a world that forms and communicates meaning. C. S. Lewis wrote such narratives in the twentieth century with his Narnia stories, as did J.R.R. Tolkien in *Lord of the Rings.* In the

Genesis creation stories, God invites Adam to name all the animals of the earth. This is more than an exercise in imagination and creativity. God is asking Adam to participate in creating a narrative that forms the meaning and place of animals in the world. Through language, Adam is invited to become a co-operator with his Creator in the ongoing emergence of creation.

As a narrative or story is formed, a tradition emerges that frames meaning and relationships; it describes how human beings and all creation interact and relate with each other. By this naming, Adam and all his descendants could make sense of their world, communicate common experience, and live in a story that took them somewhere. All this is the function of language and narrative.

We don't create the world anew with every generation, but we do change its reality. In MacIntyre's analogy of the stage, we are born into narratives and traditions that are already in progress. We learn their language and in so doing take on and are formed by the meanings that language creates. Each generation receives and transforms that tradition through interaction with its time and place. Language and narrative are never static; they're dynamic and always changing yet connected to and dependent on their tradition.

Missional congregations are formed out of the interaction between the Christian narrative in which they live and that has been passed down to them, and their listening interaction with the narratives of the people in their community. But if congregations no longer indwell a scriptural narrative memory, if the formative stories are thin and opaque to the point of having little power to inform our experience, then they have limited capacity to engage the situation they confront. If a congregation no longer has the language to name the narrative controlling it, the congregation is held captive by what it cannot name. What cannot be named is unknown; what is unknown controls us. This is the experience of the majority of people in our culture: they have lost the capacity to name the world confronting them.

An example in a local church may illustrate something that is happening at so many other levels in our culture. In one congregation a group of parents sought to protect their children from what they perceived to be the negative influence of books in the wider culture. These parents came together to demand that the local Christian school remove a list of books from its library. When the school librarian resisted, the parents escalated the struggle by going to the school board and threatened to pull their children from the school. The issue was not about books in the library, though, because this Christian school carefully monitored library acquisitions as well as the books children checked out. They also had a policy where parents could state which books they had concerns about. These books were often placed on a list that was closely monitored by staff. The books in the school library became the focal point for Christian parents who found themselves in an increasingly pluralist community with many competing values and attitudes. They could not name the deeper source of their anxiety. For example, how do we form a cohesive community of identity and belonging that shapes our children within the narrative of Christian life? So the parents reacted to a symbol (the books they primarily wanted out of the library were Lewis's Narnia series and Harry Potter). Responses of this kind come from people who feel their narrative world is under attack but as yet have no alternative language with which to engage what is actually happening to them.

An increasing number of people, including those who populate our congregations, neither live within nor are shaped by any specific narrative. When narratives erode and social context moves into rapid discontinuity, people feel as though they have no way to make sense of their experience. They lose direction, order, and purpose. A congregation becomes a receptacle for anxious individuals seeking solace and security, rather than a community that can participate in forming kingdom witness.

Innovating missional congregations begins by engaging this lived experience to invite the people of the congregation into a journey of reentering and rehearing the biblical narrative and its implications for being God's missionary people in their own situation. A missional community of this kind is formed out of the actual lived experiences of the people in the congregation. The Incarnation of our Lord declares that the place where God meets us in Jesus is not the idealism of dreamed-about ideas and principles. Jesus comes among us; the birth narratives are not intended to idealize Jesus' birth, irrespective of how we turn them into stories for our own emotional and romanticized needs. These narratives take pains to describe the ordinariness of the people and the struggles of their social reality (a census under a Roman governor, the fear of finding a place to stay because of the immediacy of birth). The narratives of Jesus' presence among us start among the ordinariness of people's lives. Jesus begins with their lived experience; he enters those experiences weaving God's story through their lived stories. He draws people into a new imagination about the nature of the good news he incarnates. Missional leadership is to be incarnate and contextual in this sense. Leaders need processes that create an open space, allowing people to engage each other in the reality of their situation rather than in idealistic, Platonic ideals of missional church or programs based on tactics or strategic plans from above.

The Missional Change Model offers a process designed to assist congregations in entering this critical place of dialogue and discernment. It is based on the assumption that if God's Spirit is among God's people, then a people must be invited into listening conversation and dialogue around their current lived experiences.

One group of congregations on the eastern seaboard enjoyed a long period of success and growth over several generations. They were proud of their identity as a contrast society. For a long time, they were aware of the slow encroachment of the city into their once-rural farm culture. By the turn of the twentieth century, they sensed themselves becoming an island in a sea of change. They sent their leaders to training programs in evangelism, church growth, and church planting, only to see most of the new congregations they planted leave them as soon as they became viable. The people of these congregations were confused and hurt. They didn't know what to do next and felt they had tried every strategy available to reach the new people in their communities. As we began meeting with the congregation we invited them into the processes described in this model. We helped them listen to the deeper, underlying fears and anxieties that were driving their agenda. We invited them into fresh ways of indwelling the Scriptures and, out of that, new ways of initiating experiments in change they discovered among themselves. These congregations gradually became aware that the underlying issues had to do with their identity as an ethnic church. Some are now engaged in experiments helping them rediscover the core of their Christian identity beyond ethnicity and how their part of the Christian tradition could help them engage their rapidly changing communities.

The next section presents the key methodologies that underlie the model. This material gives leaders an understanding of the framework shaping the model.

Congregational Lived Experience *and* Participation

Beginning with the lived experience, a congregation cultivates its participation in the emergence of missional imagination. Participation does not mean involvement in something already planned for them by their leaders, but involvement in action emerging from among them. This is why leadership is about cultivating an environment that can call forth this kind of imagination.

Cultivating environments requires processes that create the space for people to develop the ability to listen to one another and ask questions: What are the forces shaping our experience at this moment? How do we give language to what we are experiencing? How are these forces affecting our lives? How do they relate to God's narrative as we encounter it in Scripture? How are these forces shaping our lives as a congregation? As people are invited into a listening conversation that calls forth their own lived experiences and indwells the biblical narratives, out of this listening engagement emerge dreams and experiments about what God might be calling them to be as missionary people in their communities.

One of the most influential thinkers on participation is the Brazilian educator Paulo Freire. He saw existing educational systems focused on what the professional educator knew rather than on the educator's ability to create a participatory community of learners where people discovered answers to the challenges they faced. For Freire the shift to this participatory model required educators who could create an environment where dialogue among people could flourish. In his view, participation leads to the emergence of new futures.

The dialogue and participation Freire described involved people helping each other articulate their lived experiences and bringing those experiences into dialogue with Scripture. In the context of Latin America, Freire did so among the poor in urban and rural situations. His method was deceptively simple. He invited them to share the experiences of their everyday lives and then brought these stories into conversation with the Scriptures. From this they began to talk about alternative ways of addressing their challenges. From this way of being together as a people, many poor people found new ways of forming communities of hope.

Freire's pedagogy was based on the conviction that the Spirit of God is among the people of God. What Freire's method did was create an environment within which people themselves might experience the work of the creating Spirit of God and articulate specific local responses. This process empowers people with the means to listen to one another; name their own sense of what is happening to them and where they find themselves; and, through engagement with Scripture, discover how God calls them to action. Missional transformation develops around people participating and engaging with God rather than trying to convince people to get involved in someone else's solutions.

Safe Space *for* Discovering Truth Together

Parker Palmer's *To Know as We Are Known* touches on aspects of participation. In a chapter called "To Teach Is to Create Space," he describes settings where student and teacher are invited into obedience to the truth they are discovering together. For Palmer, this involves three engagements: openness, boundaries, and hospitality.

Creating space with openness requires the ability to remove the impediments and barriers that may keep the truth from seeking us out. The community itself often creates these boundaries, as when church organizations create a tacit cultural commitment not to express the fears and anxieties they feel, for concern that such feelings question core beliefs or values. To the extent these boundaries are present but unaddressed, they become so ingrained and habitual they're no longer recognized as boundaries. People become bound by social realities they cannot name, and at the same time by a church environment's tacit code that keeps them from articulating what people are experiencing. People assume these barriers are communal norms. Missional leadership involves recognizing these barriers and facilitating articulation of habits and practices that block the capacity to name what is actually being experienced. As we will see in the next chapter, the Missional Change Model constitutes a process naming the barriers.

For people to be able to participate, they need to know the boundaries in a situation. Nothing in life is without boundaries. All organisms must function with boundaries that define who they are, within set limits and expectations. There are also such boundaries in the church. They include our commitment to live in, under, and through the authority of Scripture, the particular ways in which a tradition shapes its organizational and liturgical life, and the specific social context in which a congregation is located. All of these are the givens or boundaries that shape the conversation.

Totally open-ended exploration leads only to confusion and chaos. In the classroom, an effective teacher forms a class around a set of norms, a series of boundaries that, like the membrane of a living cell, are both protection from the outside and the means through which learning and change occurs. Leaders help cultivate participation by articulating the boundaries within which the people of God operate. Once people understand the boundaries that form them as a congregation, their creativity, learning, and participation can be unleashed.

The third important ingredient that Palmer identifies is hospitality, the practice of receiving another person as a gift without the need to make him or her into something after one's own image. When leaders operate from the false assumption that they know what is best for the people, that they have a wonderful plan for the congregation's life, they develop mechanisms to convince people to accept and follow their plan. This is the opposite of the hospitality that is essential to forming a missional congregation.

Hospitality creates a safe place where people can risk expressing their experiences, emotions, and concerns about being the people of God today. In a hospitable environment, we can speak the truth about our anxieties and the confusion of living in a strange world where the meaning of being the church is obscured and the language we use no longer fits our experiences. Hospitality and participation invite us into a space where we begin learning to rediscover the narrative of the One among us calling us to an alternative journey.

This chapter has described the background of the Missional Change Model in terms of adaptive changes moving through our culture. Chapter Five describes the model itself. It is based on our practical experience working with congregations and denominational systems as well as more than forty years of research.

CHAPTER 5

The Missional Change Model

CHANGE RARELY HAPPENS IN A STRAIGHT LINE. It resembles the path of a sailboat tacking into the wind as it travels toward its destination. The path of change looks like the illustration in Figure 5.1.

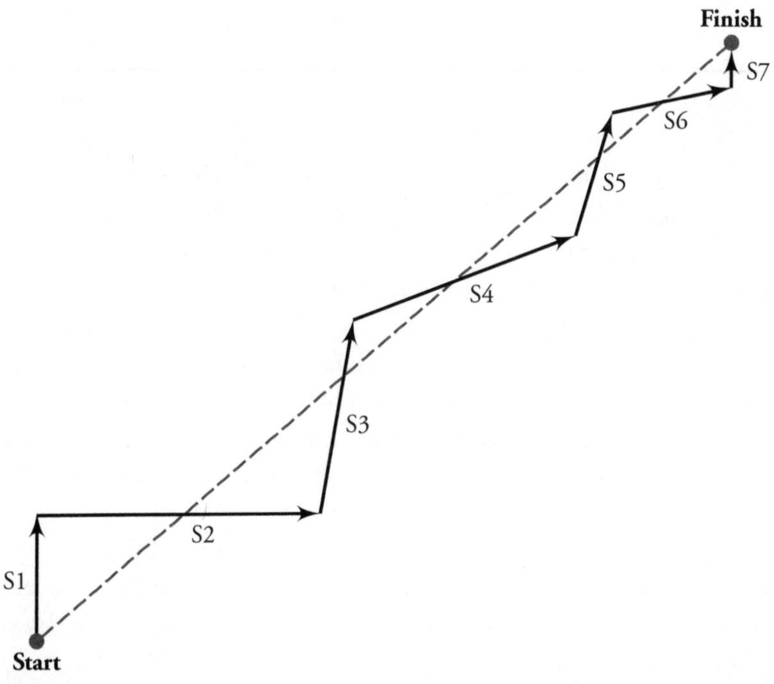

Figure 5.1. The Path of Change.

In this image, the sailboat must move back and forth to catch the variable winds that move it forward. Although the navigator has a good sense of the general direction toward the destination, he or she needs considerable skill and knowledge to read the winds and currents to reach it. The drawing represents an ideal illustration of sailboat navigation; the reality may be quite different, including getting deluged by a wave.

There is a significant difference between sailing and innovating a missional congregation: a sailor already knows the destination. But from everything said to this point it is clear that this is not the case for a transforming missional church. This is why the familiar methods of strategic planning and alignment around vision and mission statements are not too helpful at the outset. They do have a place, but not at the beginning of a process for innovating missional change. Several critical factors come into play when we're learning to sail the waters of missional innovation in a context of discontinuous change and the social and cultural contexts we discussed in Chapter Four.

First, the target is not always where we think it is; the actual shape and actions of a missional congregation are difficult to bring into focus at the beginning of this process. Just as in learning a new skill or sport (mastering the infamously hard golf swing), when we have to learn to integrate a series of new skills and teach our metaphorical arms to move in new ways, local churches and their leaders at the beginning do not clearly understand the requirements and activities of forming a missional congregation. The nature of a missional congregation and the particular activities of missional life for a local church do not usually turn out to be what we thought they would be at the beginning of the process.

Second, we will make a lot of mistakes along the way. Some of the biggest mistakes involve the ingrained habits of believing we can control outcomes on the basis of past successful experiences. This is why the process is built on the capacity to iterate small experiments directed at key adaptive challenges that the people of the local church recognize for themselves. The Missional Change Model explains how the experiments take place. These capacities give the congregation and its leadership the space to learn, adjust, and discover appropriate ways to move forward.

Third, the target keeps moving. Since our community and the context of our congregation are never static, missional engagement and missional formation are moving targets.

All of this leads to the important insight that innovating a missional church is like sailing a turbulent ocean:

- We can't assume that we know the destination before getting there.
- Since the reality of our context is shifting, the direction and nature of engagements keep shifting.
- Leaders require a new set of skills and capacities to navigate these waters.

Sources *of the* Missional Change Model

The Missional Change Model is the framework for navigating these new waters.

One important resource on which the model is based is *The Diffusion of Innovation* by Everett Rogers. Rogers is an anthropologist who has devoted his life to researching the question of how change takes place in a culture. His research shows that innovation and integration of a new idea in a system happens according to a particular pattern. Navigating toward becoming a missional congregation, even if it is obvious and advantageous, is a difficult process.

Most new ideas, plans, and strategies fail to change a congregation. The history of such change is cluttered with an endless series of plans, programs, and visions that died in birth, shortly thereafter, or as soon as the current leader left the church. This is testimony to a history of deep pain in the lives of people who sought to initiate change, silent testimony to the unarticulated loss of hope residing in many leaders. It also represents the deep, inner sense of hurt and struggle in the hearts of many who tried valiantly to create something new only to see it resisted and cut down by a congregation's ability to resist change. It is no wonder that many leaders are discouraged about the possibility of substantive change. Rogers's insights, drawn from forty years of research, help us to understand the key elements in getting change adopted in a system. Those insights are also an important part of the five steps of the Missional Change Model.

Rogers's contribution is a model of the stages of successful diffusion of innovation:

1. Knowledge. People are exposed to the nature and function of the innovation as well as to the changed context that requires innovation.

2. Persuasion. People are given the time and context that allow them to form a favorable attitude toward the innovation. They cannot simply jump over into a new idea; it is difficult to move from a reactive zone to an emergent zone culture. They need time to build confidence in both leaders and process before being willing to trust change. Transition issues must be addressed before people are ready to act in a new way.

3. Decision. People decide to commit to an innovation in their own way. It is important to learn about those ways.

4. Experimentation and implementation. People learn to put the innovation to use and thus initiate new emergent zone practices in their congregation.

5. Confirmation and reinforcement. As people continue to practice implementing an innovation, they grow in their ability to function with new practices; they come to recognize that they are operating in a new way. The continued positive outcomes embed themselves as new habits in the congregation.

Rogers's research was broader in scope than this brief summary. His work forms the basis of what follows for introducing and embedding missional transformation into a local church. Rogers's model suggests there are five stages a local church needs to move through to cultivate a missional community. Our model is designed around the steps suggested by Rogers. It is based on the assumption that, like sailing the winds, change is never a straight line. Each of the elements of the model is therefore illustrated in the context of sailing the winds (Figure 5.2).

In the Missional Change Model (or MCM), each step builds on the one before. To introduce and explain the model, we present it in

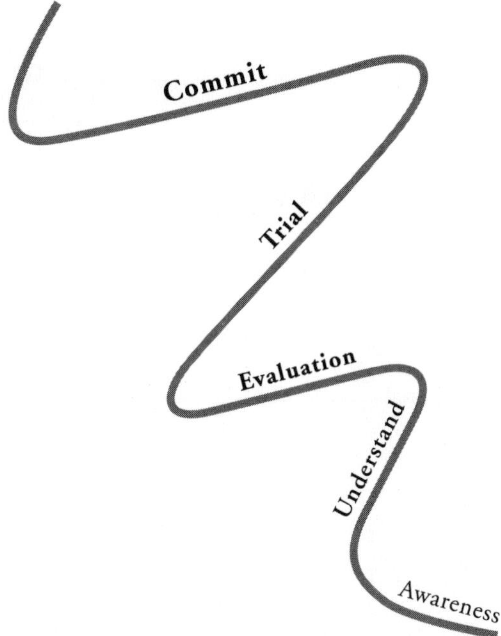

Figure 5.2. Five Elements in Sailing the Winds of Change.

linear fashion, somewhat like climbing a set of stairs one step after another. There is another way of understanding the model, through the theory of emergence described in Chapter Three. Complex systems emerge through a bottom-up process as they move from a simple level of organizational life to more complex ones by following some simple rules. Higher complexity emerges as more people get involved by following the set of rules. The actual practice of missional innovation look more like sailing the waters than climbing a set of stairs.

The model is designed with these principles in mind. In Figure 5.3 it is shown as linear steps to introduce leaders to the process by first following all the steps. At the beginning, skipping a step subverts the process. As the process is learned and more people become involved, it becomes less linear and more like sailing as the congregation learns to go back and forth across all the steps. After the congregation has gone through the process once, their movement is more like a series of spirals within one another, not a single, one-way, straight line.

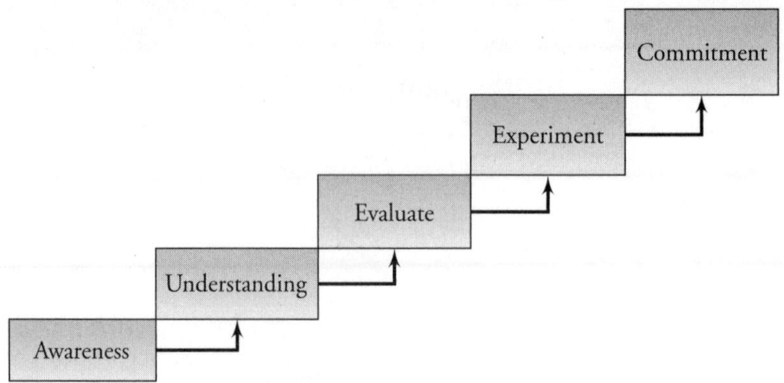

Figure 5.3. The Missional Change Model.

The Model

This chapter describes each step in the MCM, which is also the way missional leaders can help a congregation move from a performative-reactive zone culture to one in the emergent zone.

Step One: Awareness

We begin where people are at this moment.

A group of nongovernmental agencies working among semi-nomadic tribal groups in sub-Saharan Africa attempted to address a critical shortage of food and the impending threat of starvation by introducing a new form of hybrid corn that would thrive in the area's parched soil. Another group spent time with carefully developed visuals teaching women in a different tribe how to boil water, explaining why it was crucial to their children's survival. Neither initiative succeeded. What went wrong? After a series of failed efforts to fix the problem, the aid workers discovered that, in the case of boiling water, a series of cultural values in the tribal community stood in the way of the women choosing to boil water. Similar factors surrounded the issue of seed planting.

As a result, the aid workers decided on a new tack. Rather than presenting an already established solution, they began spending time with members of the tribe, listening to how the tribe formed ideas and values about being a people, and discerning how those values affected the workers' proposals for change. In other words, the aid workers were seeking to become aware.

Time and again, they discovered that this listening and awareness process revealed unexpected ways of addressing the challenges using local, internal solutions rather than external, high-tech solutions. In the case of the hybrid corn, aid workers observed that some individuals in one nomadic tribe were better nourished than others. When they sat with these people and listened to their stories, they discovered they ate root vegetables high in nutritional content that could grow in a dry climate. The aid workers then assisted tribal members to communicate this information to others, thus passing on a set of new habits for growing food that emerged out of local knowledge rather than expensive outside sources.

A similar process can be used in congregations. At a weekend conference on the church, change, and mission, a woman in her late seventies said she had never been able to understand why, after faithfully taking her children to Sunday School, they had all left the church in their late teens, never to return. Her grandchildren had no connection with the church at all. Others in the group nodded in agreement, their body language suggesting this was a common theme. The conversation quickly moved on because people were unsettled by this woman's comment and began asking more questions about what it means to be missional.

After several minutes, Alan stopped the process, turned to the grandmother who had made the comments about her grandchildren, and asked her if he could comment on the issues she had raised. She agreed and looked at him with some curiosity. He said to her, "You know, you're asking why the church in which you placed your trust failed your children. But at another level what you want to tell us is that you're in a lot of pain because your children and grandchildren no longer go to church, and that's a place of deep loss for you! Is that what you have wanted to say?"

The woman turned away with tears running down her face and said, "Yes! That's been my pain for such a long time. How could I have failed them so much?" The room fell silent as others experienced similar feelings and emotions. Their pain was real; they did not understand why their children and grandchildren were not a part of the church. They had never had permission to talk about these feelings.

They had gone to church to listen to sermons, study the Bible, volunteer for programs, and pray for one another. There was never a place where they could talk about the things churning inside them. All the questions about loss, history, and memory—their lived experience—didn't seem to have a place for expression. That lack of expression continued to cause a deep, unexpressed grief. Alan's question and the woman's willingness to speak of her experience raised everyone's awareness.

In another example, a congregation's ministry staff wanted to change the church into a missional community of the Gospel. They found that despite all their carefully developed plans, including a long process of establishing core values and a vision statement, the congregation remained unwilling to engage in the plans the team had led them into accepting at a congregational meeting two years earlier. The ministry team was confused and frustrated by the lack of congregational response to their carefully laid plans. This wasn't the first such situation. A few years earlier, acting on what seemed to have been the congregation's approval, they had brought a set of proposals for constructing a new worship center to attract a younger generation. The decision seemed sure to gain easy approval, but it was soundly defeated by the membership. The team members were confused. They didn't understand what had happened and felt betrayed by the congregation.

This example illustrates a common issue that we encounter when working with church staff on issues of change. In developing a change process in a congregation the tendency is to start with a goal or conclusion in terms of a plan, mission, or value statement. This team's instinct was to begin with a strategic plan that mapped its preferred future as a missional church. They assumed that once they had the plan, they had only to manage the stages for moving the congregation to this predetermined future. These leaders believed they were serving the congregation and leading God's people faithfully and effectively because they were acting from the habits and assumptions in which they were trained. But their genuine efforts to effect meaningful transformation were being thwarted. Their understanding of the change process did not fit the reality of the context. They were applying performative zone skills designed for a predictable, stable environment to a situation that was anything but predictable or stable. They lacked the framework to address the challenge of adaptive change. In such a setting, the congregation feels as if it is drifting in an unknown, uncontrolled direction. They see that actions and strategic plans no longer bring expected results.

These leaders became anxious and confused because they couldn't explain what was happening. They are in fact cultivating a new *awareness,* and they experience it as scary and threatening. Here are a series of words and phrases that pastors and executives used at a conference about change and mission:

Dissonance!
How do you get a handle on this?

I don't get what's going on.

Leadership is all a mish-mash for me right now.

I don't know what to do anymore.

My congregation doesn't want to hear me say that we have a lot of struggling to do, and I don't have the answers.

Give me clarity!

These leaders are aware of the feelings, but they don't yet have language to engage what lies behind the feelings.

For people in our congregations, the world is spinning. So much is happening but they have little space to process their experience and give it meaning. They come to worship with many questions and feelings that never seem to get addressed. People sense something is wrong with the state of Christian life but don't know how to express that feeling. They don't know how to articulate what lies beneath the diffuse anxiety and can't put words to the confusion. In response, leaders often make the mistake of assuming that they should address such feelings with some new strategy, plan, or program.

Nothing could be further from the truth. Until people can put their feelings into words and be heard, they are held captive by unarticulated anxiety. Leaders must create a listening space to allow people to become aware of what is happening within and among them. Such awareness requires cultivating an environment in which people discover the language for talking about what they are experiencing.

Awareness parallels the early chapters of Genesis with their focus on the "deep," the turbulent chaos over which the Spirit of God broods in the process of calling forth the creation. That calling forth happens when God speaks forth into the unformed and calls order and form into being. As we discussed in Chapter Four, the language of naming is what gives form to chaos. This form then gathers and becomes Creation, which is more than a metaphor. Creation, including the creation of human beings, is God's speech act. Thus, in the second set of creation stories God invites Adam to name the animals of the earth. As they are named, the animals come into relationship with each other. It is communication among human beings on the basis of their relationality that engages the issues of awareness. God's speaking the world into being tells us that above all else creation is about relationality. This is what God is about in the creation narratives. Relationality underlines what is intended in the description of Jesus as the Logos—the Word—of God. In Jesus Christ, God's Word, as the creative, incarnational speech-act of the Creator, is about the process of new creation. Therefore giving something or someone speech, giving words to an experience or an unformed feeling, can foster relationality and transformation. Until then, unspoken feelings and anxieties act like a powerful, dominating control mechanism. They are like the unpredictable chaos out of which anything can emerge not as relationality but as dominance and control. One clear way church leaders experience this is when they are counseling a couple around marriage issues. In this case there is often confusion and misunderstanding between the couple about what is happening in their relationship. One of the roles of the counselor is to offer language that gives them insight into the source of conflict or distress. As the words are given there is often a moment when new understanding develops and the couple feels as though something has been unlocked and they can move forward.

A similar experience happens at the level of a community of people as they struggle with issues and meaning and try to understand a changed situation in which they live. A wise leader in a congregation that had more than 150 years of history was aware that the people were struggling to understand their place in a rapidly changing community. All around them now were strange faces as people from various ethnic groups came to live in their community. The new people didn't act in the ways that had shaped the traditional habits of this community. They drove to distant malls to shop, they worked miles away from home, and they went to the theater or golf club on Sunday rather than church.

The leader saw his congregation's confusion and frustration. In response, he began to find new language to help them understand what was happening. He tapped back into their own tradition and reintroduced the language of strangers, aliens, and immigrants. He pointed out that the language they themselves used was an ethnic language once brought from another country which the newcomers around them would never understand. He then began suggesting a different language they could use to understand themselves in this new context. The new people moving into the area were themselves now like aliens and immigrants in a strange context. Out of the congregation's own past, how might they respond to such people? Through this process the people of the congregation began looking at the new people moving into their area differently. They were gradually learning how to listen with new ears and see themselves through the eyes of these strangers.

In a time of discontinuous change, language becomes frayed and stretched beyond its original meaning. People are confused as their words and the realities they observe lose congruence. When experience becomes disconnected from language, assumed meanings disappear. This can happen with unexpected, unwanted experiences such as the church community finding itself surrounded by strange, new people who have no connection with their story or tradition. Initially the people of the congregation have no words for what they are experiencing because the words that worked so well for them inside the world they created do not make sense of the new reality. Without words, people have little or no capacity to explain, understand, or begin to participate in shaping a meaningful response to the new reality.

Similarly, in local churches across North America a growing number of people are experiencing the powerful effects of worldwide change. The old language cannot give meaning to globalization that results in downsizing and outsourcing, threats of new nonpolitical groups such as terrorist organizations that can strike anywhere at anytime, or the confusion of pluralism that says the people next door are good moral Moslems whose family life outshines anything in the local church. Without a new language to connect congregation members to their traditions, these experiences will remain dark forces. The congregation needs time to begin working through its experiences of all these changing forces and to develop new language to help them imagine fresh ways of being God's people.

Awareness develops by being able to speak about where the people of God find themselves in terms of their real lived experiences at this moment. In fostering an environment of awareness, people have time to live into their feelings and tensions long enough to be given (or to evoke) words and meanings that articulate and give form to what is happening. This takes time. The ability to cultivate an environment of awareness depends on the degree to which people trust the leader's motives and maturity.

Awareness requires capacity and skills from leaders ranging from communication and teaching to listening and dialogue. The ability to communicate and teach people by using words, images, and media helps them develop vocabulary and a framework for talking to one another about their experience. The leader must be skilled in sharing information, pointing to things happening in people's lives or in the larger community, and connecting them with the experience of people in the local church as they listen to Scripture together. This involves addressing a number of questions:

- How do we listen to one another to hear what we are actually trying to express or say about our current experiences and understanding of what is happening in our lives?
- How can we explain simply, in a nonjargon way, the myriad changes occurring in the world about us that seem confusing right now?
- What kind of people do we need to be, with and for one another, to allow expression of feelings of anxiety, confusion, and struggle?
- What is it about the changes we are all experiencing that makes them so hard for us to understand or deal with right now?
- What is the difference between change and transition? Why is it so important to know this difference today?

- Where does the biblical imagination give us language to talk about what we are experiencing? What might that language be, and why is it important for us to enter it?

Awareness must be fostered all the time, but it is crucial in the transition from the reactive crisis zone to the lower performative zone. Until they have gained awareness, people cannot commit to change. Commitment is the first step in innovating a missional congregation.

Step Two: Understanding—Using Dialogue to Integrate Thinking and Feeling

One winter afternoon, we were involved in a congregation leadership retreat. Outside, the temperature was supposed to have been below zero, but instead it was nearly sixty degrees and the sky was beautifully clear. Inside, forty to fifty lay leaders were discussing the congregation's future, a difficult conversation because its glorious past was only a memory that haunted staff and parishioners with present failure for not living up to a time long past. As in many congregations, they knew the key to rediscovering vital missional life lay in shaping alternative futures, but their emotional loyalty lay with the memory of a wonderful past.

As facilitators, we wondered what it would be like to spend the day inside when the weather called the audience and us to be outside. How would we keep their attention on tasks when they had given up their only free day of that week? This day was planned as part of a series of conversations designed to engender awareness. A number of people throughout the congregation had completed our survey on elements of their life relative to missional innovation. The gathering this day was to discuss the myriad issues arising from the survey responses. One finding was that clergy were not communicating well, and the congregation was frustrated and angry. A second revolved around perennial worship wars. No one was happy with the compromises forged recently to keep as many people as possible happy. So we were gathered to teach these leaders how to have a dialogue around their awareness of these findings.

By 3:00 P.M. one might assume everyone would be tired and wishing they could leave, but the energy in the room was as high as in the morning. There was excitement, laughter, and a relaxed sense of participants invited into a space for something rare: talking creatively with one another but not getting lost in conflict.

These people were so energized and engaged because they were now aware of these major issues through finding words to describe their experiences. We had invited them to talk and listen to one another, addressing the worship issues by giving them a language other than that of individual wants or tastes, and then giving them space to dialogue with one another using this new language. By late afternoon, staff and lay leaders were having a dialogue about the overarching communication issues. Everyone felt comfortable talking about feelings (the clergy were trying to browbeat people into doing things) as well as content (how to look at communication differently).

The most significant moment, however, came when two people, one in his eighties and the other in her twenties, began talking to each other about Sunday worship. The young person was in pain because most of her peers had left her church to go to another church where the worship was more energetic and livelier. The senior was in pain because his worship had changed too much. They were shouting at each other through their hurt; both were able to express strong feelings and thoughts.

Silence fell over the room as everyone stopped to listen to the dialogue. They recognized that for the first time they were engaged in a significant conversation about something that really mattered to them, though before this conversation they hadn't known how to talk about as an issue. The congregation was beginning to shift from awareness to understanding.

This story clearly shows that as important as awareness is, it is only a starting point. Further dialogue bringing together feelings and thoughts is needed if awareness is to deepen into understanding. In the Missional Change Model process, understanding occurs when awareness enables people to ask new questions about what is happening relative to what they have been feeling and thinking. This is a time when people need to gather additional information, try out ideas, and receive feedback so they can check and orient their growing awareness and develop a new kind of knowledge base for ongoing dialogue with others. This is similar to a novice sailor learning how to tack by using the sails and rudder. The sailor learning this skill is moving beyond simple awareness that the sail and rudder need to be used together to a deeper understanding how and why they work.

The processes for gaining understanding require a good deal of attentive listening for dialogue participants to hear the underlying questions and issues that people bring up in their attempt to get vital information. As questions emerge people need to dialogue with one another, go deeper into the issues, and explore the meaning of what they are learning through face-to-face interaction. In performative zone and reactive zone congregations, communication usually narrows to the point where only close friends, members of committees that have been together for a long time, or people with similar outlooks and views interact. This is a thin environment for dialogue.

Understanding is not about developing solutions, although it is a great temptation to think so. In an atmosphere of the back and forth of quality dialogue, people want to go quickly to solutions. But solutions at that point are premature. In fact, pursuing a solution thwarts achieving full understanding. The purpose of understanding is to take awareness deeper and test a new explanatory framework. Most people need a lot of time and space to talk about a missional congregation before the ideas take on a workable meaning. Simply using the words or giving people essays to read does not develop the level of understanding they need. The process requires dialogue that goes over the same material, but each time the richness of the understanding deepens and broadens.

While flying cross-country once, Alan opened the airline magazine. He saw a large full-color image of a tree and its root system below ground. What was riveting about the image was that about 80 percent of the picture was the underground root system; only 20 percent was the visible tree. The point was that most of what really makes a difference is going on under the ground, out of sight. This image helps to clarify the difference between awareness and understanding.

Awareness is analogous to developing language that makes it possible to talk about a tree and make sense of it in this context. But it's impossible to really understand what the tree is about without going underground and examining its roots, which are the true life source of the tree. Similarly, if we too quickly assume we know what is happening in the lives of our people or the larger community in which the church is located and hasten on to plans and solutions, we are only addressing the tree we see above the ground. We're missing almost all of what is actually happening to people, and our action will tend to be misdirected. Understanding is the capacity to go beneath the surface of what usually passes for dialogue and resist the desire to jump ahead to the solution. Understanding begins to deepen appreciation for what is actually being said and experienced. This level of engagement leads people to the next stages of the process and guides them toward new experiments in being God's missionary people in their community.

During the understanding process, the experiences and language formed in awareness are framed into more helpful explanations. New questioning stimulates new forms of thinking. The congregation gains clarity on the issues it faces. People struggle with whether tried-and-true formulas for action are appropriate to what they are discovering. After the eighty-year-old and the twenty-year-old in the anecdote met in dialogue, the man took three weeks away from his regular church attendance to visit a local Vineyard congregation in a town where the young adults had gone. Thanks to his dialogue with the young woman, he wanted to understand more. This act of servant leadership created its own space for others to continue the dialogue by listening more intently and striving to understand the real issues to be engaged.

The understanding process in the Missional Change Model is not completed in one meeting. It's an ongoing dialogue in which people find the space to ask questions and explore the emotional and affective implications of awareness. We cannot stress enough how important it is to take time with this process. Awareness and understanding are like gestation and birth. There must be a long time period for life to be formed, and in most instances the birth requires its own process. The leader is like a midwife assisting a birth process that must follow its own mysterious ways. If the ground is prepared and the leader cultivates the proper environment, shaping a space rather than forcing a strategy or plan, the process of missional formation will encourage a congregation to organize itself and change will emerge.

The stages of awareness and understanding can last from six to twelve months in the initial process. But in another sense, these two stages are happening all the time as people move back and forth in conversation and engagement around various developing challenges to mission that they encounter in a changing context. Once understanding has grown and deepened, it is time for evaluation, the next stage of the change model.

Step Three: Evaluation—Applying Awareness and Understanding

Forming an emergent zone, a missional congregation requires that awareness and understanding connect with evaluation. In this third stage, which can last from three to six months, people apply their understanding and growing capacities to engage in dialogue about what is happening in the congregation and in social and cultural contexts. During evaluation the congregation examines current actions, attitudes, and values in light of new understanding. People can now consider whether specific activities, programs, and commitments are congruent with their awareness and understanding of missional innovation and the context in which they find themselves. They begin asking questions:

Is what we are doing congruent with how we now understand our context and ourselves?

What new skills or attitudes might we need to develop, given what we're learning?

What other groups might already be working on ideas or actions that help us think through what we need to do?

Where does our growing understanding of being a missional church rub up against our current practices of life together?

Why do we keep functioning in certain ways that we know are counterproductive to being a missional people?

Which elements of our tradition are of great service to us, and which do we need to rethink?

What new information do we need to make good decisions about some of our current programs?

Are current budgeting processes helping or hindering our new understanding?

What new skills must we develop to effectively engage this context?

Are the expectations we have of our leaders empowering them to form us as a missional people?

Which are the areas they must focus on, and which must they set aside in terms of priority?

As awareness and understand engage the congregation, its desire for actions increases. This is not the time for action and planning, but evaluation. At this stage, it is vital for members to take the time to evaluate their current activities, attitudes, and values as a congregation relative to its changing context. People need to ask about the support they need in terms of skills, structures, and resources to move forward. The congregation is now also in a decision-making phase, discerning whether to choose to move forward with deliberate actions for missional innovation or to halt the process. The congregation moves toward or away from actions that will effect change and mission. Again, as with the other processes in the MCM, it is vital to take time and not rush evaluation. As in the understanding phase, people want to develop action steps, but it is critical to stay in the evaluation phase long enough to ask questions and assess current realities. As important as it is to get into action and solution, if a congregation does not take enough time for awareness, understanding, and evaluation then most solutions will yield only a short-term burst of hope and energy, but then the congregation will return to its previous state.

The evaluation process can create anxiety. People are now poised to engage in actions that will change a lot of past activity and move into an unknown future. What is required from leaders in this phase is clearly and frequently communicating that the congregation is not going to choose wholesale change but is going to learn how to develop a missional future by taking small, significant steps. People have to be reassured that much of their congregational life will remain fairly familiar, and there will be no structural and organizational changes. Rather, they should know that they and their leaders are going to discern some creative experiments to address the real, critical, adaptive challenges in becoming a missional community. The leader's role is to create a holding-tank environment in which much of the regular life of the congregation continues, but some critical experiments are also initiated that can show people another kind of future that may be developed. From there, the congregation can move to experimentation.

Step Four: Experimentation—Risking Some Change

This is the stage where the congregation can test new ways of shaping its missional life. When people practice and experiment with what they have been learning, real cultural change can be embedded in their lives as a congregation. How experimentation happens is as important as the fact that people are ready to engage in change.

An example of an experiment involved a group of several newly retired seniors who sold their large homes and moved into an adult community in the deteriorating neighborhood around their church. This neighborhood had become an island of white members in an increasingly multiracial community. With fresh eyes, these seniors saw how they could improve conditions in the area, but when they went to neighborhood associations with proposals they were met with mistrust and resistance. One storeowner on the main street told these "do-good white folk" to get out of his store.

At first surprised and discouraged, the seniors decided they needed to try an experiment. Every Tuesday and Thursday they walked the main street of the neighborhood picking up rubbish, which they packed into bags and took away. After some twelve months of faithfully following this routine, several of the seniors were invited into the store of the owner who, the previous year, had told them to leave and not come back. Thus began a dialogue and friendship built around questions of how to serve their community together across racial differences.

This is an illustration of people in a congregation initiating an experiment in serving their neighborhood, but the same dynamic is true of change proposals inside a congregation. Churches in the performative or reactive zone are often suspicious of any large-scale proposal to reorganize structures and programs to bring about change, whether missional or otherwise. They find a way to resist no matter how well conceived or well intentioned the proposal might be. A congregation that has operated for a long time in a performative zone culture sees a large-scale change proposal as highly disruptive to long established habit and practice. It is difficult for most people to imagine what such change might look like or achieve because they are so embedded in their performative zone culture. So they resist. Similarly, in the reactive zone, anxiety is already running at a high level, and the trust quotient is low. In this situation, the best-developed plans run afoul of people's feelings of confusion, anxiety, loss of trust, and inability to imagine how to act differently from what has been the norm.

How leaders handle experimentation is critical to missional transformation becoming embedded in the congregation. At this point in the congregation's life, it needs what writer and leadership expert Ron Heifetz describes as *adaptive* rather than *tactical* change. The goal is to introduce a process that invites people into changing the *culture* of the congregation, not just its programs or organization. As Heifetz says,

> The importance—and difficulty—of distinguishing between adaptive and technical change can be illustrated with an analogy. When your car has problems, you can go to a mechanic. Most of the time, the mechanic can fix the car. But if your car troubles stem from the way a family member drives, the problems are likely to recur. Treating the problems as purely technical ones—taking the car to the mechanic time and again to get it back on the road—masks the real issues. Maybe you need to get your mother to stop drinking and driving, get your grandfather to give up his driver's license, or get your teenager to be more cautious. Whatever the underlying problems, the mechanic can't solve them. Instead, changes in the family need to occur, and that won't be easy. That's because even those not directly affected by an adaptive change typically experience discomfort when someone upsets a group's or an organization's equilibrium.[1]

Tactical change is about taking action that improves what is already being done in the congregation or favoring action that has always been used but is now being applied to fix the new challenge. This is about changing programs, introducing new programs, or changing elements of the organizational life of the congregation. For example, because a performative zone congregation has lost the world of loyal customers, it experiences increasing loss of income and a budget deficit. A tactical approach is to cut staff and use undesignated bequests to cover the shortfall. The finance board or the senior pastor might use the Sunday morning service to exhort members to give more as a sign of commitment and faithfulness. This is a tactic that misses the fundamental nature of the challenges facing the congregation.

Tactical change assumes that the same approach that has always been used will solve the new challenges. The congregation members know who lives in their community. They can even name the changes in population that have occurred over the years. They are aware that what they are doing is no longer reaching the community. But when asked to imagine what they might do, their response tends to be of a tactical nature. They suggest building a new sign on the front lawn of the church building, refurbishing a hall as a youth drop-in center, replacing the carpet in the sanctuary, and so forth. Their imagination is shaped around what they have always been doing and how to improve these activities in the hope of being more effective at reaching people in the changing context of their community.

Adaptive change requires us to design a new approach to the challenges we face. Late performative zone and reactive zone congregations are in a situation where taking the car back to the mechanic one more time is not going to address the critical underlying challenges. They have to make adaptive changes. But adaptive change is the kind that congregations strongly resist. This is why they don't need another overarching strategic plan to bring about change in the church but instead need what we discussed in Chapter Three as *emergent* change. It is about encouraging the congregation to develop multiple forms of experimentation.

The retired couples in the changing neighborhood are an example of adaptive change. They discovered that imposing ambitious plans for change on their neighbors would not work. They began what we call "experiments around the edges." They did not try to overwhelm or force change on people who were not ready. They started an experiment that was nonthreatening to the community of racially mixed people who suspected the intentions of white, middle-class folks. They did it without fanfare, and in fact without having a grand plan to change other people. They simply started an experiment in making a difference that did not claim to have all the answers or indicate they wanted to control all the outcomes. For a long time, they went about their quiet, unpretentious experiment. Every week, whether in sun, rain, or snow, they picked up trash off the sidewalks. Gradually things began to happen. One woman said that when she first moved into the community, she went into a store owned by a black leader in the community. She wanted to talk with him about the neighborhood, its needs, and how it might be changed. He ignored her. When she persisted he reluctantly talked with her but made it clear that she and others like her had nothing to contribute. Months later, she met him again on the sidewalk outside his store. Now he was curious, open for conversation, and ready to talk with her and others about larger questions concerning the neighborhood.

This story is not unique. We are beginning to understand that the anomaly was the long historical period of performative congregations. The problem is that when we come to evaluate what we should do, the only solution many of us know is tactical, performative action, such as command-and-control or strategic planning. But there are examples that help us imagine what emergent experimental processes might look like in cultivating a missional congregation.

John Ellis's Pulitzer Prize winning book *The Founding Brothers: The Revolutionary Generation*[2] illustrates the experimentation stage. The book is about the men who participated in forming the American nation. As Ellis points out:

> The creation of a separate American nation occurred suddenly rather than gradually. . . . No one present at the start knew how it would turn out in the end. What in retrospect has the look of a foreordained unfolding of God's will was in reality an improvisational affair in which sheer chance, pure luck—both good and bad—and specific decisions made in the crucible of specific military and political crisis determined the outcome. . . . The basic framework for all these institutions and traditions was built in a sudden spasm of enforced and makeshift construction during the final decades of the eighteenth century.[3]

He argues that it was neither grand vision nor a big plan that formed the American nation but a group of men who, in the exigencies of a moment filled with great stress and without any clarity of outcome, instigated a series of experiments that began to form the nascent republic: "The real drama of the American Revolution . . . was its inherent messiness. This meant recovering the exciting but terrifying sense that all the major players had at the time—namely, that they were making it up as they went along, improvising on the edge of catastrophe."[4]

Then there is this observation:

> For [John] Adams, the American Revolution was still an experiment, a sail into uncharted waters that no other ship of state had ever successfully navigated. There were no maps or charts to guide republican government claiming to derive its authority and legitimacy from public opinion, that murky source of sovereignty that could be as choppy and unpredictable as the waves of the ocean. He had been a member of the crew on this maiden voyage, even taken his turn at the helm, so he knew as well as anyone, better than most, that they had nearly crashed and sunk on several occasions, had argued bitterly among themselves throughout the 1790s about the proper course.[5]

This is how effective, lasting missional transformation starts to happen in a performative-reactive zone context. It cannot be done by large-scale plans imposed on people. It is done by initiating all manner of experiments around the edges where people are given permission to try out what they are learning. These experiments are not about creating permanent change. They are about testing and discovering along the way. The beauty of such experiments is that, like the wind of the Spirit in our sails, there is no telling where they'll take a congregation.

One cannot predict up front what such experiments will do to people's imagination. They give the congregation a chance to test new skills and try new ideas. People can grow an emergent zone sensibility, learning organizational skills that can emerge without having to bet the congregation's whole life on their outcomes. But as the initial experiments bear fruit, others in the congregation begin to see that it is possible to imagine and practice new habits and actions without destroying what they know and love. This encourages increasing confidence in the change process and starts to change the culture of the congregation, gently shifting it from a reactive or performative zone toward an emergent zone culture. The process takes time, but it embeds new habits and values in the congregation from the bottom up rather than the top down.

In one congregation we know, a woman in her sixties was part of such a process. She was invited to participate in a group looking at the question of how the various generations in the congregation might understand one another and be God's people together. The team moved through the stages of awareness, understanding, and evaluation. They were now ready to initiate some experiments in response to their discovery. During a weekend meeting, she came up to Alan with tears in her eyes. "There has been a lot of change around this church," she said. "But it's been a whole lot of the leaders coming to us and telling us how we need to change and what we need to do. The changes have been done to us, and I've been very angry for a long time. I had lost hope in this congregation ever being any different!"

Then her countenance changed, a smile came on her face, and she began moving her arms together to signify a bottom-up process. She said, "I now have hope, I believe we can make this church a great church for the Lord because we are being given the resources and tools to make a difference rather than being told what to do."

This woman became an ambassador. She talked to many of her friends of the same age who felt profoundly marginalized by all the top-down change. Her hopeful message was that it was possible to be different and learn new ways of being the church. It was something they could learn to do with and for one another. Like the eighty-year-old who went off to the Vineyard church to discover why all the young people in the congregation were leaving his own, her experiments around the edges began to change the culture of the congregation's life. It takes time, but it also makes long-term cultural change possible. Without the time for experimentation, there can be no missional transformation.

Step Five: Commitment—Signing on to New Ways of Being Church

Finally, as the experiments gather more people, the confidence of the community grows. They believe they can become an emergent zone congregation. This is when a missional culture is embedded in the congregation not as the idea of one person, not because of the personality or power of a specific leader, but because the people themselves have taken on a new way of being church together. People have internalized the framework of missional life.

There is a lot more to the Missional Change Model, but this chapter has given an overview to show how it works. A key question for leaders contemplating moving through the steps of the model, however, is whether the congregation is ready for this kind of change and innovation.

Readiness *for* Missional Innovation

We know that within a congregation people are ready for change at different times and rates. Therefore it is important to understand how the MCM builds on this readiness to change and innovate. The speed with which people adopt new ideas follows the pattern shown in Table 5.1.

Given that only 10–15 percent of any group has low resistance to change and are ready to adopt innovation, an attempt to innovate missional culture in a congregation that tries to begin with universal agreement (usually around some unknown and ill-defined concept) is headed for failure from the start. The key to initiating missional change is to begin with that first 10–15 percent of innovators. Leaders should direct change efforts for the first eighteen months at getting about 10 percent of their churches or system members through the stages of the Missional Change Model and into the commitment stage. It's difficult and rare to reduce this time frame.

Awareness takes about four to six months. A useful rule of thumb is that if you start with 50 percent of the people in a congregation in the awareness stage, you will lose 10 percent at each successive stage of the change process. The 10 percent left are the innovators because they are the people who will start the missional change process.

In the second eighteen months, the first 10 percent who become committed will take the next 15 percent, the responders, through the

TABLE 5.1. *Change Adoption Categories.*

Percentage of People	*Degree of Resistance*	*Readiness for Change*
10	Low	Innovators
15	↑	Responders
25		Adapters
25	↓	Joiners
15		Resisters
10	High	Laggards

five stages of the change model. Note that the people, not the leaders, make this happen. In many studies, researchers have found that it was necessary for those committed to a new idea or concept to actively dialogue with others to create a higher level of commitment. The discussion and sharing of the first 10 percent with the next 15 percent takes the next group through the process. At the end of three years, about 25 percent of the congregation will have moved to the commitment stage. Once a congregation reaches this level, the change process can't be stopped because it now has a momentum and life of its own.

During a third eighteen-month period, 50–65 percent of the remaining members will go through the stages toward commitment. The rate of missional change accelerates as more and more people get on board. However, this is an unsettling time because 10–25 percent of the people (the so-called resisters and laggards) will fight change and actively resist. Some of them will not accept the change and leave. Their departure creates a crisis for leaders in terms of how they will manage their own anxiety and conflict issues as laggards and resisters try to maintain the status quo. We have discovered that those are the leaders who cultivate basic Christian disciplines such as prayer, daily Scripture dwelling, the practice of listening, and discernment. Leaders whose lives are embedded in the practice of Christian life and a community of prayer and conversation are best able to sustain themselves during this period.

Summary

Here is a recap of the Missional Change Model, its steps, and what happens in each step (Table 5.2).

The MCM offers leaders a way to cultivate an environment in which missional imagination can thrive. Leaders must be able to function in an ambiguous and uncertain environment. They are men and women capable of practicing local missional theology. The significance of missional theology throughout this process cannot be overstated. The leader moves back and forth across these stages as people raise their questions, make new discoveries, and shift in their biblical imagination. This is the wonderful work of a leadership that creates the space for people to dialogue, evaluate, and experiment within a field of rich biblical and theological dialogue.

TABLE 5.2. *Recap of the Missional Change Model.*

Stage 1: creating awareness	Through intensive communication events, both one-on-one and in groups, leaders take people through dialogue and discussion about the need for missional transformation of the church.	4–6 months
Stage 2: creating understanding	The dialogue and discussion serve to bring thinking and feeling modes of understanding together into a coherent pattern of understanding.	3–5 months
Stage 3: evaluation	What is currently happening in the congregation is evaluated in light of awareness and understanding.	3–5 months
Stage 4: creating experiments	People begin to identify actions that they believe will move them toward becoming a missional church. The critical word is *action.* People will experiment through action.	3–8 months
Stage 5: commit	People commit to getting others involved in the process of moving through awareness to understanding, to evaluation, to experimentation, and finally to commitment.	

Getting Ready *to* Lead Missional Change

The Missional Change Model is clearly not a quick fix, like taking the car to a mechanic or creating a tactical solution to the challenges of discontinuous change. The MCM is designed to assist leaders in cultivating an environment of adaptive, emergent zone culture in their congregation. Skills for leading a congregation in this missional transformation are introduced in the next chapters, but first let's take a brief look at how leaders can get ready to cultivate missional change in their congregation. The stages suggested here are useful in exploring the skills and capacities of missional leadership described in the remaining chapters.

Step One: Take Stock of What You Know

The missional leader requires a well-developed understanding of the environment in which congregations now function. It involves not only knowledge of missional ecclesiology but also the changed situation of the church vis-à-vis the shifts reshaping the social and cultural context of our time. This is ongoing work that requires study, discussion, learning, and reflection. Figure 5.4 suggests the nature of these challenges.

Step Two: Know Yourself as a Leader

The second stage involves taking a snapshot of who you are as a leader at this moment and how others perceive and experience your leadership. There is no substitute for direct, clear, and honest feedback. The majority of church leaders have had no such feedback on their leadership for a long time, if ever. Lack of performance feedback is a powerful limiting factor in being able to identify the new skills and capacities needed to develop a missional congregation or missional capacity for yourself.

The best way to get this feedback is through a 360 degree instrument, which asks a cross section of people with whom you are work-

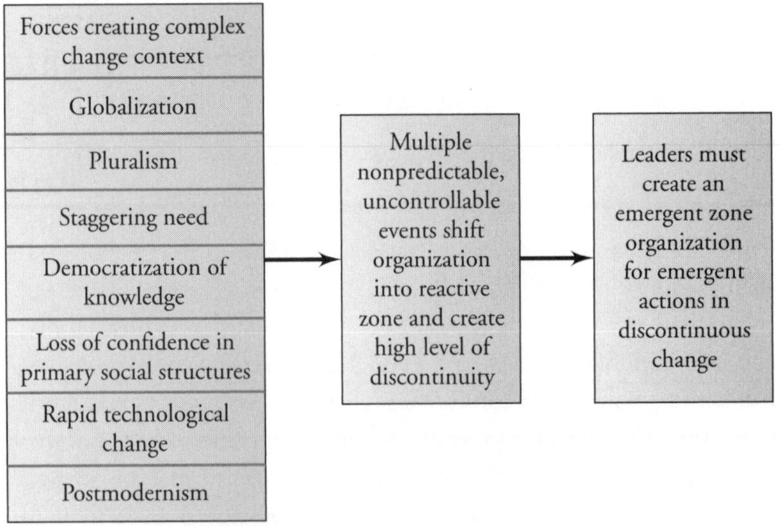

Figure 5.4. Responding to Discontinuous Change.

ing and among whom you are pastoring to evaluate you as a leader along several dimensions. The instrument assists you in identifying your leadership readiness for missional change. We have seen this process repeatedly offer the most powerful and effective means for leaders to begin assessing and dialoguing about their leadership readiness in terms of missional transformation. This kind of evaluation does not measure standard pastoral leadership capacities because to a great extent those capacities were developed for performative zone congregations. The instrument to be used identifies skills that the pastor has or lacks for leading a congregation through discontinuous change and directing the members toward an emergent zone organizational culture. Information on how to obtain our 360 degree survey can be found in the back of this book.

Step Three: Listen

Rather than immediately seeking solutions to fix areas needing leadership development, we ask leaders to spend time actively listening to trusted friends, colleagues, and mentors to ask them a series of questions. Listening takes time and involves readiness to hold off on the urge to jump to a solution. Listening is about willingness to go deeper into the questions of how people perceive and experience your leadership, to develop a clearer sense of the key areas for change and development. For example, we work with leaders to identify several areas for leadership development. We then create a series of questions around each area and design a listening process whereby leaders can go deeper into understanding what people are observing and can give them feedback on their leadership readiness.

Step Four: Focus on Key Areas and Issues

Toward the end of the listening process, the leader focuses on several specific areas of leadership capacity as the key ones to develop in terms of missional skills. Our instruments evaluate a range of readiness capacities, but we recommend a leader begin by focusing on only the two (three at most) critical areas identified through the listening process.

Step Five: Develop an Action Plan

Once the key areas have been identified, leaders need to design a clear, intentional learning path to develop the identified skills over a twelve-month period. The plan includes several elements, such as identifying the kind of training required, where the training can be gotten, how it will be done within the leader's schedule, when the training will take place, and who else might need to be involved. Most leaders tend to design their professional development around current strengths so as to concentrate on what they are already doing well or what catches their interest at a particular moment. Our action plan takes leaders into a zone of personal discomfort where they need to risk learning unfamiliar skills, habits, and capacities that they are often afraid to address. This process takes courage. A second element in the plan requires leaders to identify specific action areas where they actively experiment in using these new skills. In this way, new skills gradually become embedded in the leader's toolkit as normative habits and practices.

Step Six: Commit

This is a journey without a destination. In discontinuous change, there is an ongoing need to keep getting clear, hard-hitting feedback from trustworthy mentors and colleagues. The commitment to continue the 360 degree process places leaders in a process where they can assess their skills regularly. In this way the leader models an essential element of an emergent zone organization: a culture that is always open to self-evaluation, creative learning, and willingness to risk new development amid dynamic, unpredictable change.

We strongly recommend that in reading the next chapters you keep these six key stages in mind and begin thinking how to apply them to yourself in your context.

PART 2

The Missional Leader

CHAPTER 6

Missional Readiness Factors and the Nature of Leadership

In many workshops pastors tell us about the strain of the demands that their congregations are making of them. One pastor phoned Alan recently and described how fifty people had left the congregation because he was initiating the changes they had asked for and agreed on. "What's happening?" he asked. He was struggling because he thought he'd been doing exactly what the congregation hired him to do. He carefully obtained their approval before moving forward with the changes. But six months into the process, the system was in an uproar as these fifty people left the church and others suffered the pain of the loss.

Another pastor told us how his aging congregation expected him to fix the decline and budget shortfalls by becoming an entrepreneurial leader like those they'd read about in books on churches successfully turned around. The pastor was also in great pain because he knew he was neither wired to be that kind of leader nor prepared for demands of this kind when he began ministry twenty years earlier. Like many pastors we meet, he was deeply anxious because expectations of his leadership so dramatically changed. He wanted out of the church to which God had called him but didn't know what to do. He was caught in a spiral of demand, accusation, expectation, and feelings of failure.

In the reactive zone, congregations demand more and more from their leaders. They want them to "do something" about their discomfort or confusion or whatever is happening in the church that creates anxiety. Like the pastors in these stories, many leaders are struggling to know how they can adapt, what skills they must have, and how to address their own deep sense of inadequacy and anxiety. They need concrete resources to cultivate effective, lasting missional transformation in the congregation. Essentially any leader can acquire the tools and skills to lead a missional church. This chapter explores the key readiness factors we have found to be important for leaders wanting to innovate lasting missional change.

Missional Leadership Readiness Factors

Recall the six-step process for cultivating missional transformation that we discusssed in Chapter Five:

1. Take stock of what you know.
2. Know yourself as a leader.
3. Listen.
4. Focus on key areas and issues.
5. Develop an action plan.
6. Commit.

Using this process helps you understand the importance of feedback and how to identify where you can begin to cultivate new capacities for congregational missional transformation. Rarely do church leaders have the opportunity to receive the gift of feedback in a form that clearly identifies ways to engage the missional challenge facing them. The Scottish poet Robert Burns once wrote: "O wad some power the giftie gie us, to see ourselves as others see us." Leaders know well that although they may receive abundant praise from those who love them and criticism from those who are never satisfied, it is a true gift to receive feedback about themselves as leaders. Such feedback is fundamental to the other processes of readiness for cultivating a missional congregation.

We have identified a series of readiness factors for cultivating the missional congregation. Most planning and leadership skills pastors learned were designed for a performative zone context where linear, developmental change made it possible to predict and plan a desired future on the basis of what happened in the past. For example, they would develop a strategic plan with three-to-five-year goals around mission and vision statements and then align resources around the plan and measure progress toward the goals. These leadership skills and capacities work poorly in the transition from reactive to performative to emergent zones.

The readiness factors we have identified are based on the assumption that most church systems must be led through a turbulent zone of discontinuity and transition where the emerging context can be neither defined nor controlled. Innovation and leadership capacity are required. Some readiness factors are not new, while others will be new to the congregation. However, they are framed and presented in a new way from the perspective of a missional ecclesiology. These factors represent the beginning of a journey of analysis and discussion that can result in a picture of leadership radically different from the one you were given in school or learned by watching other leaders. Taken together, these factors begin to describe the shape and work of missional leadership.

The Interplay *of* Personal Attributes *and* Missional Readiness Factors

Cultivating a missional congregation requires skills and competencies that combine personal attributes and specific readiness factors. These attributes and factors differ from the standard set of pastoral skills taught in seminary. Skills in pastoral care, worship, preaching, and organizational management are important, but they must be reinterpreted in light of a missional context of rapid, discontinuous change. They must be understood less from a performative perspective than from the emergent. Figures 6.1 and 6.2 introduce a framework of these attributes and factors. The factors and attributes are addressed separately in following chapters.

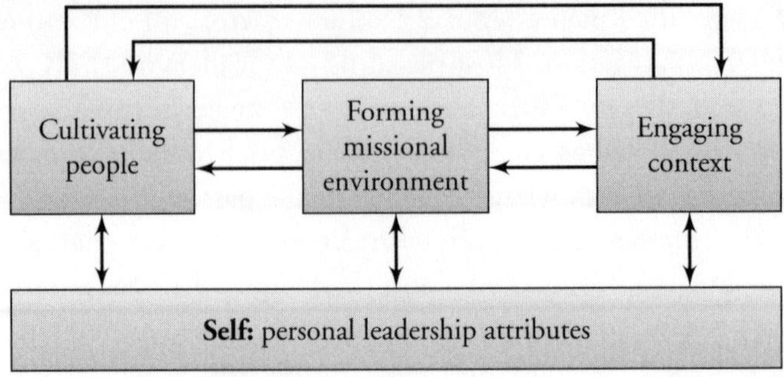

Figure 6.1. Personal Attributes and Readiness Factors in Missional Leadership.

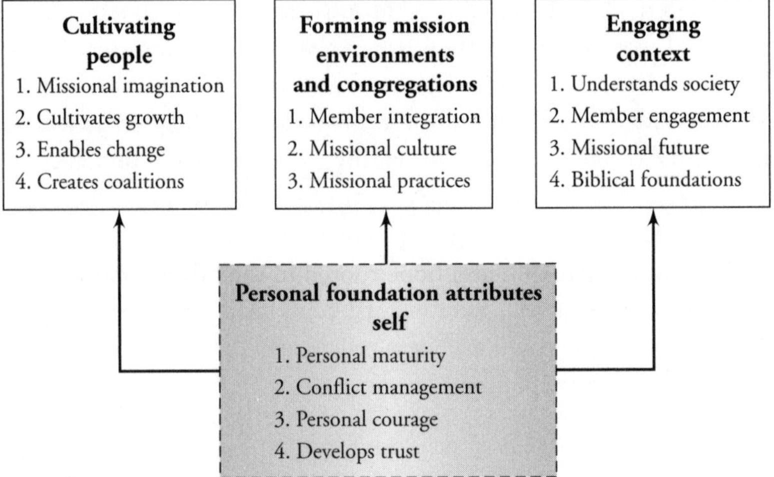

Figure 6.2. Interaction of Personal Attributes and Congregational Readiness Factors.

The diagram shows four interconnected areas in which leadership must function to innovate a missional congregation.

Self: Personal Leadership Attributes

The primary element in cultivating a missional congregation is the personal character of the leader, those traits and habits that must be present if anyone is to lead an organization through adaptive, discontinuous change exiting the performative zone. This is the area we describe as self-identity.

Self-identity is the foundation on which everything else is constructed. Missional leadership depends on the leader's maturity, trust, and integrity. Well-developed capabilities in the other three areas are important, but they support lasting change only if the congregation has a high level of confidence in the leader's character. These attributes are placed first because they are the ticket to missional leadership.

People: Attributes for Cultivating People

Innovating the missional imagination of the people of God requires leaders with the capacity to form a community in which people are able to hold listening conversation with one another at the level of awareness and understanding.

Our second level of focus is the skill of cultivating conversation, more so than skill in organizational or strategic planning processes. If God's imagination for a congregation is among the people then they are the source (and resource) for the congregation's missional imagination. Leadership is therefore about this capacity to cultivate conversation of imagination and hope rooted in the biblical narratives, but without manipulating people into a prearranged plan or prepackaged program.

Congregation: Attributes for Innovating a Missional Environment

An important capacity for the missional leader is the ability to mentor and coach people into some of the critical practices and habits that form the character and identity of a Christian community: dwelling regularly in the Scriptures; cultivating the habit of listening with the desire to hear the other; regular practice of keeping a daily office of prayer, Scripture, and silence; and regularly giving hospitality to the stranger. The missional life of the people develops through these habits and practices. Such practices and habits are essential for developing an environment out of which a congregation learns to discern the ways God may be calling it into new and imaginative forms of missional life. Again, this is not primarily about organizational structure but instead the leader's ability to model patterns and habits of life. Rather than focusing on reorganizing structure or polity, we focus on developing these practices as key leadership skills.

Context: Attributes for Missional Engagement

Missional leadership is also about the capacity to develop a continuing relationship of awareness and understanding with the people, neighborhood, community, social reality, and changing issues in which they are located. This is what we mean by context.

Every congregation is embedded in complex social interrelationships of pluralized and often fragmented neighborhoods, work environments, and relationships where multiple stories compete and coexist with one another. This is a new world for the congregation, and leaders need to direct their energy to forming a witnessing community that learns to experiment with fresh ways of being God's sign, witness, and foretaste of the kingdom in their multiple contexts.

The next chapter presents a profile of each attribute or factor and its characteristics. The remaining chapters of Part Two function like compass points indicating the direction in which the leader must sail to be an effective "orienteer" or "navigator" of God's people. We hope the chapters constitute a unique map to help you understand how to grow as a leader in cultivating a missional congregation. But before we move forward to that discussion, we want to address some important concepts about the nature of leadership itself. How is being a leader in a church—missional or not—different from being a leader in any other setting? Before looking at these issues and questions, let's step back and take a more global look at the notion of leadership.

The End Toward Which We Must Move

In some circles, there has been concern about the very use of the word *leader.*[1] Without engaging in a lengthy discussion, we offer some observations about use of the word. Through much of the twentieth century the dominant images and metaphors used to describe and define the nature of leadership in the church have been borrowed and carried over from other arenas such as business, without much critical reflection. Indeed, much of the discussion apparently assumed that leadership in the church is the same as in most other areas of life and work.

A common, uncritical assumption is that because *leader* is used with congregations and other organizations, the characteristics and skills are pretty much the same for them all. There is some validity to this assumption. For example, in this book we assume a congregation must function in a pluralist context of rapid and major discontinuous change. We believe that many of the insights and lessons learned about how to lead in these contexts have important implications for congregations. In the same vein, the congregation today is a complex organization. It is no longer situated in a small, agrarian community or emerging merchant town of the sixteenth century, when the dominant modern models of congregational life were formed. The congregation must now function in a complex sociocultural matrix requiring organizational and management skills that can't be ignored or spiritualized away. In our experience, many congregations are in trouble because their leaders don't know the most basic principles of leading people, forming effective staff, developing teams, or communicating processes. Crucial to forming missional communities, these skills are aspects of leadership that can be learned in other settings.

Nevertheless, leadership from the perspective of forming a missional congregation also differs from the case of other organizations and communities. This difference involves the purposes that shape the leader's activities. Aristotle wrote about understanding the nature of something by asking about its *telos,* or end. This is more than asking what someone or something does in relation to other activities. It is not purpose in the sense of having a function, but purpose as the end toward which it must move. So we must ask, What is the end toward which missional leadership ought to move? Why do we function as leaders in that community called the church?

In the Christian story, the *telos* of human life is neither to fulfill oneself in the modern sense of the individual nor the drive to self-actualization or even self-differentiation. Our *telos* is to know God. Both Augustine and Aquinas state that it is God who is our end, and therefore our source. To know God is to know the Good. Knowing God is also participating in a life infused with proper calling, and to do the work we have been given to do in this life. Only by participating in the life of God can we live out our *telos* and live into our work and purpose. By doing our proper work in life, we know happiness in the sense of knowing God. As human beings our quest for the Good is a quest for the *telos* of our life, which can only be known in God.

This is not a "spiritual" idea. It has practical, concrete implications for who we are and how we lead; it has everything to do with answering questions about the nature and meaning of leadership in the church. Before anything else, leadership is about our identity as people who are participating in God's life and given work to be in done in the world. Leadership is about identity formed out of knowing the *telos,* which in turn can be known only from participating in the life of God. Therefore leadership is fundamentally about forming character and living a life shaped by virtue.

At the core of leadership, then, is the question of one's identity and its source. This is why the church cannot simply borrow its categories for leadership from other arenas and impose them on its life. To do so is to borrow a purpose and end that are not shaped out of this fundamental participation with God. When we borrow from other arenas such as business or corporate governance, we actually form a character and identity as a leader that, though it may be successful by any number of measurements, leads away from formation as God's person. It also gives the church that is involved a distorted understanding of itself and its own purposes. For example, some current leadership models derive from measuring effectiveness in terms of numbers and size, which are not necessarily measures of success in a life with God.

Instead, the question of leadership formation must be asked *only* in terms of what God is doing in forming the social community known as the *ecclesia.* Responding to this question requires looking at matters of theology, specifically the incarnation of Christ.

The Theological Roots *of* Christian Leadership

When we read how early leaders of the church wrote about their tasks—that is, the *telos* framing their activities—it is clear that they understood leadership differently from how we understand it today. In the second century, Tertullian exemplified an understanding of leadership that seems startlingly absent from contemporary discussion or practice. His engagement with issues of the church's life, identity, and practical direction emerged from his theological perspective. This understanding was that in Jesus Christ, the God of Abraham, Isaac, and Jacob (Israel in all its concrete history) was forming a new society in the world. There were now a new people, an alternative community with a new citizenship. Tertullian's theological understanding shaped his actions as a leader as well as all the practical questions about how to lead the church. He led on biblical and theological convictions about how men and women are formed into an alternative society in a world shaped by Caesar. The implication of this theologically focused worldview was that leaders were to be preoccupied with forming a people, with ways of socializing new believers into a new society that was the church. Today, in discussion about the nature of church leadership, there is little theological wrestling with the questions of how to form or socialize a people into an alternative community. On the contrary, there is growing emphasis on how to help seekers feel they belong in a congregation without any expectations or demands on their lives.

It is a strange twist of thinking to watch this kind of conversation. In the time of Tertullian, someone wanting to *belong* to the church had to go through a rigorous period of training focused on behavior (how daily life was actually lived). In other words, to belong to the new community of Jesus, a person was mentored in practicing change in habits. Today leaders talk about the need to create a safe, nonthreatening, low threshold of belonging in order to draw people into the church. Note the two radically different ways in which the same language is being used. These approaches suggest contrasting sources of understanding. In the latter case and in our contemporary context, the source of this thinking is not a theologically, biblically formed imagination but the latest marketing strategies that come from polls and studies about what people are looking for when they want to join a group. This is not to suggest that we not seek to welcome people into our churches. It is to point out the distinct sources of our leadership imagination today.

Tertullian's primary concern as a leader was formation of a people around a specific set of habits and practices that came out of his engagement with Scripture. Wayne Meeks and others have noted that what shaped the imagination of these people and their leadership was the drive to "resocialization into an alternative community."[2] This is a missional activity focused on formation of a people as God's new society. As church historian Alan Kreider points out, this focus on formation was lost in a Christendom that continued to shape the imagination of Christian life in late modernity.[3] Kreider has examined changes in the interpretation and practice of conversion from the early centuries to the time of Charlemagne. He traces how the meaning and means of conversion shifted drastically over this period: "Conversion, which had made Christians into distinct people—resident aliens—now was something that made people ordinary, not resident aliens but simply residents."[4] As a result, the church entered the long period of Christendom and the focus of leadership shifted from formation of a people as an alternative society of God's future to oversight of orthodoxy, proper administration of the sacraments, and regulation of spiritualized and privatized ethical practices increasingly disconnected from any biblical or theological understanding of the *ecclesia* as the people of God.[5]

Within this Christendom framing of leadership came notions of proper management, along with the conception of the leader as one who makes things happen by creating change processes and who is measured in terms of quantitative growth. Growth became an increasingly significant focus of leadership in North America as the church began to lose its privileged status of primary religious option in the culture.

Leadership *and the* Incarnation

The Incarnation lies at the heart of the early church's wrestling over what it meant to be the church in specific cultures. The concrete, material revelation of God in Jesus Christ was the basis of their thinking and practice. This is why the character and identity of those leading the church were articulated in terms of participation in God. But this participation was not about some private, otherworldly, spiritual practices having nothing to do with the public, political, social life of a people. It was in fact the very opposite. Participation in God meant forming a community of God's people whose lives often challenged the political and social institutions of their day. Certainly, some of the persecution that visited the early Christians came from people who understood that Christian communities threatened and undermined the power and authority of the ruling classes of the day. The Incarnation Jesus is not transformed into a dematerialized, spiritual experience that affects only the inner subjective life of an individual.

For the early church leaders, the Incarnation was political because it made plain that the God we meet in Christ cannot be separated from the concrete realities of how we live in our particular place, time, and culture. This is political because it is about how citizens determine their relationship with one another and with the outsider. We continue to have difficulty understanding the implications of the Incarnation's concrete nature and materiality. Many others in the early centuries were not able to grasp the meaning of the fact and confession that God entered and embraced the physical, temporal materiality of the world. Gnostic movements have always sought to dematerialize and spiritualize Jesus, limiting God's engagement to some inner, spiritual experience that is disembodied from most of the public and material engagement of the world. It is easier to deal with the implications of a Gnostic, spiritualized Jesus than the One encountered through the biblical narratives and the confessions of the early church. Similarly, we are colonized by modern ideas of the two separate worlds of the practical and spiritual, the division between public and private. We come perilously close to losing the recognition held by the early church that the Incarnation not only changes everything but becomes the center from which all reality must now be understood and all of life practiced.

In the Incarnation, God meets us in the concreteness of our place and time, not in an ethereal, disembodied realm of ideas, feelings, or spirituality or the modern reductionism of Christian confession. The problem confronting leaders in forming and cultivating a missional church is that we have drunk so deeply from the well of such modern categories. We accept its bifurcation so implicitly that we function within a practical atheism, or at best functional Gnosticism, that continues to separate the material and spiritual as if they were two distinct and separate realms having nothing to do with each other. As a result, leadership practices and capacities are uncritically adopted from outside Christian understanding, while leadership character is developed from within the Christian narrative of inner, personal, spiritual life. Leaders practice this basic dualism by seeking to develop spiritual habits as part of the formation of character and then uncritically adopting leadership skills from other arenas to shape vision, create change processes, and manage systems.

The formula is a simple one: personal spirituality (the private, inner world of the individual; personal character of the leader; what we describe as the spiritual life or ethics) plus good leadership technique (the concrete, historical world that we "make" through our actions) equals a leader with character and effectiveness (ideal type).

The sources of this view are neither the Scripture nor the hard-won confessions and lived lives of the early church but the reductionism of modernity. As Lesslie Newbigin pointed out,[6] what the early leaders did so carefully and daringly was think about all of life from the perspective of God's revelation in Jesus. They did not first seek out some framework or resource in the broader culture and then justify it by arguing that it was consistent with this revelation. They went much further. They centered their understanding, framing, and practices of Christian formation (and therefore the nature of leadership) on the fact of the Incarnation as the place where God's intentions and purposes are made known.

The Formation *of a* People

The early church believed it was being formed as God's alternative community within a regnant empire; consequently, leadership was about formation of a people. We see this in how they formed new members through catechesis[7]; it was a matter of developing practices that formed people into a social community called the church, the eschatological and social order of God's reign. Leadership entailed formation of such a people as witnesses to the acts of God in Jesus Christ.

Missional leadership is not effectiveness, meeting the inner, spiritual needs of self-actualizing and self-differentiating individuals, or creating numerical growth. It is different from building healthy, nonanxious relationships among members of a congregation so that they appear attractive to people outside the church. Missional leadership is cultivating an environment that releases the missional imagination of the people of God.

Theologian Stanley Hauerwas articulates the challenge for missional leadership in these terms: "In short, the great problem of modernity for the church is how we are to survive as disciplined communities in democratic societies."[8] Modern frameworks have formed the imagination of today's church leadership. This is why leadership is viewed as shaping individual spirituality, as forming a congregation within unexamined norms for health borrowed from psychology and family therapy, as growing a congregation in size or developing a strategic plan. Absent from such a framework is a theological accounting of leadership as the calling to form alternative communities of the kingdom shaped by theological and biblical narrative. Hauerwas again offers helpful insights into what this could mean: "We are not Christians because of what we believe, but because we have been called to be disciples of Jesus. To become a disciple is not a matter of a new or changed self-understanding, but rather to become part of a different community with a different set of practices. . . ."[9]

Such formation calls for leaders who themselves have been apprenticed in the art of formation in the alternative society of God. These leaders are in short supply within Protestant North America. Instead, we see a rising demand for the leader as entrepreneur (to make things happen and drive for success), diagnostician of health (the church as doctor or therapist), or grower of homogeneous gatherings (forming gated religious communities in anxious suburban worlds). There is a dearth of those schooled in the practices of catechesis, confession, hospitality to the stranger, forgiveness, and shaping life as a Eucharistic community.

A Relational People

The Incarnation compelled the early church to confess something that went against people's most basic intuitions about the nature of God, and it became the crucial, revolutionary experience of God. Their encounter with Christ compelled them to confess that God is Trinity. From this Trinitarian understanding of God came their understanding that all reality was neither Greek neo-Platonism nor Eastern forms of dematerialized spirituality, but God in relationship with men and women. The One who encounters us in Jesus is the God who is relationship as Father, Son, and Spirit. God called into being a creation that reflects God's nature. In the New Testament and in the early church, this meant forming a people in a new community that reflected in its life together the nature of God. The church was the sign, witness, and foretaste of God's life in the future of all creation.

Missional leadership is about cultivating an environment in which this relationality of the kingdom might be experienced. The gift of the Spirit means the church is the place where we are invited to risk, in relationship to the open-ended adventure of the Spirit's presence.[10]

Leaders cultivate an environment in which the boundary breaking Spirit constantly calls forth new ways of being God's community. Missiologist David J. Bosch describes Acts as the story of how the Spirit breaks the boundaries of planning and expectation of the young church. Things just don't turn out the way the early leaders plan. They are drawn into a journey that didn't fit into their categories and plans. The church is not something we make or compel to happen. We do not plan its emerging future; we do not define it in a vision statement that can be realized through a controlled and managed strategic plan. The church's future is elicited from among the people who make up the ecclesia. Leaders who get people to follow their strategies and plans do not build the future of the church. Missional leaders cultivate a way of life among a people through which God's future is elicited among the people. God eludes our systemizing; God's ecclesia cannot be mastered or managed or made. God gives us our future by the Spirit; we are invited to participate in the unfolding of the present and the future of the kingdom in the concrete places where missional communities live.

The next chapter presents the factors that equip leaders to move forward on this adventure.

CHAPTER 7

The Character of a Missional Leader

ALAN WAS WALKING ALONG THE SEA WALL IN Vancouver with Clark, an executive presbyter in a West Coast Presbytery. Clark was halfway through a sabbatical that had taken him to several training events in the Search Conference process in the United States and Ireland. At the same time he visited with church leaders in Scotland to learn how they were shaping a missional strategy in their context.

Clark was reflecting with Alan on how he had changed over these last three years working within the Presbytery to achieve missional change. Clark talked about the early days when, through an inventory we developed called the *Executive Leader Missional Survey,* we introduced Clark to the attributes and factors explained in this book. At many levels, Clark was seen as a leader with high integrity and maturity, but as he himself was aware, conflict and courage were still difficult areas in his leadership. Though he was able to articulate vision, when it came to cultivating people and the system itself around a vision he felt lost at sea and defeated. When he started our process, Clark was a leader with great passion for God's work and the churches he served, but he sensed his passion slipping away as his days became filled with the tasks of maintenance. His energy was shifting from the

Presbytery to a number of groups and conversations within church-wide organizations.

Now three years later, Clark remarked on how he had changed. He was leading a risky courageous process of change across the Presbytery, engaging people in processes of imagination and change that were emerging from their work together. He convinced many in the Presbytery that they didn't need to fight battles across the denomination; instead they could develop a different kind of Presbytery.

What struck Alan most about Clark's transformation was not only his confidence but his understanding of the leadership principles discussed in this book. He was calling forth God's future from among the people rather than coming at them with preplanned programs and strategies. Clark was now comfortable within a world of forming people and shaping an emergent direction for the organization. The change began with the 360 degree inventory we did of Clark as a leader. Clark had the courage and passion to listen to the inventory results, and the maturity to receive the input and evaluation of thirty other leaders who completed the inventory on him as well as listen even more deeply to what they were saying through the report. Clark's transformation began at this point. In this chapter we look at the essential factors for effective missional leadership.

The Identity *and* Character *of a* Leader

As discussed in Chapter Six, the leader's personal character, what we call self-identity, is paramount among the four attributes and factors of missional leadership. Self-identity refers to the nature, character, and behavior of a leader in relationship to the congregation and its developing life. The process of becoming a leader is no less than the process of becoming a fully integrated human being. This statement requires explanation.

Missional leadership is first about the leader's character and formation. Leaders either form or deform the emergence of the Spirit's work among God's people. The questions people in a congregation often ask, indirectly or obviously, concern whether or not they can trust their leader through change that feels risky and unknown. They want to know about the leader's credibility and authenticity. The challenge of inviting a congregation through a process of major internal transformation requires maturity and character; it demands the ability to model the values and beliefs at the heart of missional transformation.

Character is a matter of personal habits, skills, and behaviors that engender confidence and credibility. It also involves a leader's motivation, values, and sense of life purpose. Character requires self-knowledge and clear evidence that Jesus Christ is the center of the leader's life, meaning, and call. Character is the place where one's deep hunger, personal identity, and calling merge to generate the confidence that allows people to trust a leader and agree to journey together in a new direction. Such character is observed in four personal qualities: maturity, conflict management, personal courage, and trustworthiness and trusting.

Personal Maturity

Cultivating an environment where the missional imagination of the people of God can emerge requires a mature leader who is self-aware, authentic, and present to the realities and concerns of those being led. An emotionally aware and mature leader is best equipped to navigate the complexity of discontinuous change. One of Clark's outstanding characteristics was an emotional maturity that allowed him to model his own leadership development work for others. When he received his inventory report from the input of some thirty leaders across the Presbytery, he had the courage and maturity to share the results with them and talk about the places where he was genuinely struggling. This gave other leaders the confidence to enter the process and begin their own work of leadership development. Without this kind of leadership from Clark, it is unlikely he would have been able to create an opening for risk and change across the Presbytery. These people trusted Clark even though they sensed he did not have all the skills and capacities needed at that point. But they knew his heart and heard his openness and readiness to place himself in the call to change. Their trust made a huge difference in what happened in the Presbytery.

The personal maturity of a missional leader must have three main ingredients: being present to oneself and to others, being authentic, and being self-aware.

BEING PRESENT TO ONESELF AND TO OTHERS. We live in a social context that rewards leaders who achieve quantifiable, external results. Significant financial rewards offered to CEOs make them focus on increasing the short-term return for investors. Executives such as those at Enron and other large corporations in the past few years who have made morally questionable decisions and allowed unethical behavior to flourish in their organization illustrate a deep-seated cultural conviction about success and effectiveness in terms of numbers and dollars. We know that too many leaders lack an inner compass, which comes from a life given to shaping their own maturity.

This kind of thinking has also permeated the church. Pastors are increasingly pressured to be successful at growing the congregation and making it work. Many respond by denying what this pressure is doing to them on the inside. The pastors we met at a leadership conference acknowledged a growing level of anxiety and discouragement about their leadership because of pressure from their congregation to compete with megachurches. They were supposed to become charismatic, entrepreneurial leaders. Most knew they could not meet such demands but nevertheless felt pressure to perform.

In North America, success entails ability to control and manipulate the external environment to produce certain outcomes. If these external performance-based criteria become the benchmark for leadership, the cost is a loss of the leaders' own personal awareness of who they are among a group of people, how they function, and how they are perceived. Without this awareness, it is difficult to lead a people through significant change. One pastor, whom we'll call Bill, leads a midsize congregation in the western United States. In a session with other pastors, he talked of how many new members had come to the congregation through outreach programs developed over the past several years. In the next breath, he criticized other pastors and his denomination because they were not "spiritual" enough by his standards. He meant doing evangelism his way, believing as he did when it came to specific issues in the churches, and coming to his weekly prayer meeting.

Bill was woefully unaware of how he was externalizing all this conversation, measuring people by his own preset standards of what the church should look like and how the denomination ought to believe and behave. He does not comprehend that many in his congregation feel he isn't listening to them. They feel bruised and misunderstood, wondering why they continue in the church. Bill has little self-awareness and therefore little personal maturity.

The people of the congregation don't know what to do with their pastor. They are polite on the outside but dying on the inside. Bill is not cultivating the kind of environment within which a missional imagination might emerge. He has a long list of jobs and programs, but the people have little sense that their lives are valued or that their cries are heard.

This is an extreme example of a common malady affecting a lot of well-intentioned, gifted leaders. Alan remembers initiating a church restart in downtown Toronto in the early eighties. From the beginning there was pressure from many sides, even from inside Alan and from the spoken and unspoken expectations of others—to make it work and be successful.

For almost two years he and a few others worked diligently on making this restart a success. There were numerous meetings, ongoing strategies to reach people and integrate them into the young community, visits to people's homes, and efforts to make small groups effective. There was also action to find the money to pay bills and put bread on the table, attempts to interpret what was happening to others, and continuous dealing with denominational leaders who did not understand or support the changes. The list went on.

As the church restart grew and gained a critical mass to sustain itself, theirs became one of the churches to check out in the city. Week after week, Alan and his wife would entertain people on two or three nights as well as almost every Sunday. The greater the growth, the bigger the challenges, and the more strategies that seemed to be required. Something in the back of his head kept suggesting that he was so occupied with living in the externals of making things happen that he was missing a huge part of his life: his wife, kids, and a lot of people around him. But the work had to be done, and he felt that some day soon he could stop the train, take stock, and get back to "normal."

Of course, we know that this putting off has its costs. Eventually, once everyone knew the church was thriving and it was time to breathe, people would have to deal with one another and there were no resources to help them do that. It was painful to see friends part with each other as if they were strangers. Why? Largely because they focused on the externals of making things work at the expense of self-awareness and engagement with one another.

This is why the 360 degree inventory can be so valuable for the change process. In working with one group of pastors to develop the skills and capacities they needed for missional innovation in their congregations, we used our 360 degree inventory to begin a conversation among them. We gave them the opportunity to talk about how they were currently functioning in leadership and to explore the elements they would need to develop.

Chris, one of the young leaders in the group, was in his second pastorate. He had recently moved across the country after spending eight years in a small town in western Pennsylvania following graduation from seminary. The university congregation he moved to comprised some strong board members eager to share their vision for the church with the new younger pastor. Chris was incredibly mature about his leadership in the new congregation. He already understood that, for him, to get quickly on the merry-go-round of strategic plans, visioning futures, and design programs would not only be the wrong path for the congregation but the kiss of death to his spirit. He talked with a spiritual director, he joined us in multiple conversations about missional church, and he ceaselessly expressed his own anxiety about the growing expectations from some leaders that he would lead the charge on a strategic plan for growth.

Chris was aware of how his own life had been shaped by the spiritual practices described in earlier chapters. In his meetings with the board he invited them into times of dwelling first in Scripture and listening to God and one another for periods of time. He met some of his strategic planning board members for breakfast and listened to their hearts. He spoke to them about experimenting with another way of discerning what God might have for them as a congregation.

At first these board members grew frustrated with him because they wanted action and they thought he wanted only to talk. We remember conversations with him as he expressed his deep commitment to these leaders and a willingness to work this through with them despite his anxiety about their responses. Chris persisted with a gentle but firm awareness of both his own commitments and the central importance of cultivating a board willing to listen to Scripture (and one another) before running off into planning and programs.

Gradually, after about eighteen months of patient journeying in the same direction through meetings, lunches, coffee with leaders, preaching, retreats, and conversations over supper, his experiments in listening to God through Scripture and one another in their meetings began to bear fruit. There are many parts to this story, but the important point is that the gradual transformation of the leadership board into a community ready to listen to the Spirit through Scriptures and to what the Spirit was shaping among the people was directly the result of Chris's own self-awareness and maturity as a young leader.

BEING AUTHENTIC. Authenticity is a difficult word to describe, but it is mostly a matter of consistency and congruence. In *Authentic Leadership: Courage in Action,* Robert W. Terry remarks: "Many of us sense a deep, pervasive, and profoundly disturbing disconnection between the world that we experience as we actually live in it and the world that we create and describe in our rhetoric and imagination. . . . Many of us grasp the disconnection intuitively. Others search for evidence. All of us are responding to an erosion of reality. Few doubt the current rapidity of change or underestimate the likelihood of its increased acceleration. What is uncertain and unsettling is the unknown direction of that change. Is it heading for promise or peril?"[1]

Part of our new reality is the erosion of any sense of common purpose or story among people. Loss of confidence in the stories that sustained North American life in the twentieth century is accelerating. The orthodoxies of that century are less and less capable of addressing the discontinuity pressing on our lives today. The men and women who now populate the majority of congregations in North America feel the loss of direction. Only in lives manifesting a direction shaped by a common story is there any possibility of forming a people in this context. The need for leadership today is the lived, authentic demonstration of a life coherent and consistent with its professed beliefs and narratives.

The authentic leader is one whose actions and words are coherent and internally consistent. This quality communicates that leaders know we live in a time and place where discontinuity runs deep and that they are facing these issues honestly, not living in self-deception. In a culture where people feel increasingly disconnected from themselves and others, we need leaders who demonstrate a connectivity and inner consistency with themselves and others.

Tim, one such leader, lives in the Midwest. Eight years ago he believed he was being called to start a church that offered a context for honest conversation with adults in their twenties and thirties who were leaving their churches in droves. When Alan talked with leaders in this church, they described Tim as the primary reason it is now packed with nine hundred young adults every week. When Alan asked why, no one answered in terms of big plans, programs, and strategies, which in fact could have been more intentionally developed. Each leader said the reason for the growth was Tim's own character and self-awareness. He communicated with others as a person shaped inside the Christian story. He could readily admit that he did not have all the answers but was willing to listen and work with people in order to discern how God might want to shape them as a church. Young adults are drawn to this church because they sense in Tim a deeply authentic leader who is aware of the hard issues they are facing at so many levels of their lives. Tim shares his own journey and his ongoing working through of questions in dialogue with Scripture.

BEING SELF-AWARE. If awareness is the first important stage in the journey toward forming a missional imagination among people, then the leader's self-awareness is critical to the process. In the Missional Change Model, awareness implies a congregation connecting with the narratives that both form and deform the community of God's people. Leaders are crucial here. If they have not taken the inner time to understand and find language for the narrative of their own lives, they will never be able to cultivate this kind of narrative life within a congregation. Maturity means a life formed over the long journey by the narrative-shaping God.[2] It is about the character of those who have allowed God to confront their shadows. Leaders who have not plumbed the depths of their own self-awareness have neither the resources nor security to cultivate an environment of awareness within the congregation. Personal maturity involves leaders in a narrative that gives their lives a center and direction.

Chris exemplifies this kind of maturity. We are aware of how easy it is to be deeply involved in strategies for growth or even pastoral care that brings praise from a congregation. We also know that our involvement may be coming from a need to please, be in control, or be a caregiver to others—needs that the leader has never appropriately understood. Engaging in one's own self-awareness takes work; it is not done easily and requires persistence over the long haul.

Jim is such a leader. He had the courage to meet regularly with a group of coleaders to evaluate his own inner responses to the large system he is leading. He has been willing to face being driven by anxiety over not getting clear direction amid ambiguity.

Vera is an amazing leader working with a growing number of younger leaders in emergent church planting experiments in the eastern United States. By understanding the inside dynamics that drive her, she has become aware of when her work is directed toward shaping them as leaders in a situation where there are no easy or ready answers to the questions of engaging young adults who come from far outside the church world. She is able to listen to these emergent leaders, point them in a direction, suggest experiments, and walk with them without having to control their decisions or provide some plan for their lives. In her calm and steady maturity, they have found the resources to trust one another, take risks, and experiment.

Karen is another self-aware leader who is forming a missional order in the Pacific Northwest. Designated as an emergent young leader who should be watched because of her strong gifts, she is invited into many conversations among emergent leader groups. She comes into these situations as someone not needing to be in control or position herself as an expert or leader who has a lot to offer. She is quiet, watchful, confident, and always listening. Being with Karen, one has a sense of someone who is steady and has a direction, a person who will not judge and criticize others but is focused on a call. You know you are with someone whose life is centered. Karen has faced the demons of being used as a token minority person in a white church world. Nevertheless, she has not allowed that to become a negative power in her life. She is a mature leader who inspires confidence on a journey that is moving into places where few of us have ventured. Who among us has had experience as American Protestants in forming a monastic community in an urban setting? But people are ready to listen to and join Karen on this journey. Her quiet maturity plays a significant role in this leadership.

Maturity equips people with the confidence to continue even when the journey is dark or difficult. Mature leaders understand the connection between the end and purpose of their lives and the work to which they have been called. They have an inner consistency of life and work.

Few of us would rightly claim that we have become fully mature, but as a leader of a community innovating a missional imagination you need to continue growing in self-awareness, authenticity, and your ability to be present to yourself and others. Others look to you to show the interconnection among your inner identity, how you balance your life around your calling, and how you live out that movement as a leader in your engagement with others.

Managing conflict is one of the critical elements of self-awareness. This may not seem like the place to discuss conflict since handling it appears to be a skill rather than a self-awareness issue. However, our experience with leaders is that conflict management issues go to the heart of their own maturity and awareness. Most church leaders have been trained to deal with such conflict situations in the church as marriage distress or disagreement among people. They have had little training or experience in working with their own inner response to conflict in a situation where nothing is to be solved or removed but instead used to creatively engage change. If a leader is unaware of what conflict means and does for him or her personally, the leader can't engage the kind of change required today.

Conflict Management

Missional transformation puts a leader in a high-conflict zone. Being at this place involves leading people in an in-between time, when current habits and practices are increasingly dysfunctional yet the future is not discernible. Any group living with this much tension experiences significant conflict. Conflict is normal in any change process, but it must be understood and managed. Missional leaders need the capacity to put conflict in the context of change, in three ways.

CONFLICT IS NORMAL IN CHANGE. Pastors typically develop skill in minimizing dissonance. They see conflict as negative and want to bring it to quick closure. This attitude, however, is counterproductive for innovating change. Missional leaders need to be skillful in engaging conflict and helping people live in ambiguity long enough to ask new questions about who they are as God's people.

Traditionally, people were told that conflict is bad and must be rooted out of the church so that people will see Christians as different. This way of thinking and living is false in its understanding of God's purposes. The New Testament witness to the early Christians ("see how they love each other") reflected the fact that these Christians disagreed, argued, promoted divergent views of what the church should be, and were competitive and even power hungry. They did not suppress the reality of their life together but instead discovered the unity of the Spirit through their many conflicts. They loved one another in the midst of the messiness of their lives; they discovered God's community because of this reality.

Missional leaders can model ways of engaging conflict to bring about change. They must be ready to create conflict that helps people think differently, name conflict, and facilitate its resolution. They will live with conflict and still sleep at night.

NO CONFLICT, NO MOVEMENT. The negative feelings arising out of conflict with another person actually create energy that can be used to seek out that person and engage in the difficult task of conflict resolution. Conflict always produces energy, which can become a resource for resolving conflict. When we engage the conflict, we grow and our relationship with the other person becomes stronger. However, most of us have not learned to use the energy arising from a conflict positively. We can repress it and suffer myriad painful reactions. Fred remembers being in conflict with a coworker that resulted in a painful case of hemorrhoids. This person was literally a pain in the behind. Once the conflict was resolved, the hemorrhoids disappeared.

As a psychologist, Fred believes we underestimate the impact conflict has on us, every day. Long-standing, unresolved conflict can bring physical illness, interfere with relationships, and destroy lives. We have trained pastors to minimize conflict. Culture and families teach us to avoid it, neutralize it, give in to make it go away. We learn to dread conflict and demonize others with whom we differ, rather than accept and deal with the conflict.

PRACTICE MAKES A DIFFERENCE. We can learn the stages, steps, process, and inner workings of conflict resolution, but we need the actual experience of entering into the process of it to get better at dealing with conflict. Sometimes leaders need to understand that how they've learned to handle conflict can be harmful to them and their congregation. For example, we were working with a pastor team that scored low on this dimension in their Pastor/Leader surveys (see Chapter Eleven). We stopped and discussed the value of conflict. One of the pastors reacted as if a light had gone on in her head. She said, "You mean to tell me that all this time that I've been avoiding people, not returning phone calls to people that I knew were unhappy with what I'm doing, being nice-nice to people that I was angry with. . . ." She paused. ". . . That I was hurting myself and them? And I was actually getting worse at dealing constructively with conflict at the same time?"

We did not have to reply. She got it. That afternoon she began to return phone calls to a number of people she'd been avoiding. This tiny bit of knowledge about conflict was all it took for her to readjust her thinking and behavior. For many others, it takes a more detailed study of the nature, scope, and process of conflict resolution.

Jerry, for example, was invited to a small town congregation undergoing rapid transformation as Hispanic workers settled in the area and quickly began replacing the once-dominant white Anglo culture. The church to which he was called was about 90 percent white and had a long history in the town. The call committee and church board had told Jerry they wanted to change and were looking for a leader who would work with them to reach the Hispanic community. As soon as Jerry moved into the community, he began learning Spanish. He was so eager that he planned a one-month study leave in Mexico to continue developing his Spanish language skills and his understanding of the culture.

After eight months in the church, rumors surfaced that church leaders were unhappy with Jerry's activities with the Hispanic community. Refusing to believe the rumors, Jerry just kept going in the same direction. After all, he thought they told him this is what they wanted when he accepted the call.

Tension quickly grew within the church. The board called the denominational executive and threatened to remove Jerry if something wasn't done to change his actions. Jerry appeared confused when the executive met with him. By this time he had his own support in the congregation and spent all his time with these people, pleading his case and receiving their support.

We met Jerry at this time during a pastors retreat. We were working with our process for understanding conflict. We pointed out to Jerry that in the midst of significant conflict he was shrinking the circle of his own comfort zone by avoiding the leaders of the congregation and spending lots of time with those who supported and encouraged him.

The lights went on for him when he saw the picture we drew that showed how he was creating safety for himself and at the same time guaranteeing a deepening conflict in the congregation. Jerry was stunned by what he saw and realized that the picture accurately portrayed his actions. The situation had nothing to do with who was right or wrong around the issues concerning his time with Hispanic people. Instead, the problem was how he perceived and managed the conflict about his behavior. When he asked us what he should do, we described ways in which he could reengage the board and other leaders through listening dialogue. Once he began that process, the atmosphere of the congregation began to change.

In developing self-awareness, maturity, and the capacity to understand their own role in issues of conflict, missional leaders need a great deal of courage. Engaging a congregation in the difficult, ongoing work of missional change also requires a high degree of courageous choice.

Personal Courage

Missional leadership is not for the faint-hearted. It takes courage to do the right thing when it is neither easy nor comfortable and to accept the personal consequences of leading people out of familiar habits and patterns toward an alternative future. When Moses brought his people across the Red Sea, they were thrilled that someone was finally acting to free them from slavery. But once in the desert, they discovered that the habits learned in Egypt could not sustain them on this new journey. They grew angry and complained, demanding that Moses return them to the security of Egypt. He showed personal courage in his willingness to pay the price of resisting the pressure to give in to their demands.

Pastors leading missional transformation require the kind of personal courage that makes them ready to sacrifice popularity in order to tackle tough issues. Personal courage is the capacity to go on a long journey in the same direction, even when few seem willing to follow. It means keeping to one's core values, ideals, and sense of call, even if they have become unpopular.

This courage is essential as the congregation realizes that missional change is not a short-term problem solved by pragmatic programs. Instead, it entails forming an alternative imagination over time. Personal courage, however, is not the same as foolhardiness. Acting for the sake of acting is not personal courage. Acting purely on the basis of a set of ideas or hunches and intuitions about something is less personal courage and more lack of maturity. Sometimes, personal courage means willingness to discipline oneself to learn new skills and work on other readiness factors before rushing into action.

Each story in this chapter illustrates such courage, demonstrating the reality that a significant level of personal courage is needed to lead people through this kind of change. Our experience is not that leaders don't have courage; rather, they must understand some of the critical areas where they have to practice courage. For example, Jerry has wonderful courage when it comes to moving outside his own world to learn the language and customs of the Hispanics in town. The place where he needed to focus a lot of courage, however, was in overcoming his tendency to avoid confrontation, and in putting aside outreach issues to patiently and lovingly listen to anxious, angry leaders within the congregation.

There are many aphorisms about courage:

If you can't stand the heat, get out of the kitchen.

The buck stops here.

Behold the turtle; he only makes progress when he sticks his neck out.

To be great is to be misunderstood.

When the going gets tough, the tough get going.

Lead, follow, or get out of the way.

The breakfast of champions is not cereal; it's the opposition.

Personal courage can be learned and developed, but it can be realized only in the trenches of life, not in a classroom.

Trustworthiness and Trusting

Without trust, missional transformation can never occur because it is the glue that enables a community to move forward in difficult times. Trust demands communication of consistency between action and character. It is closely related to maturity, particularly to authenticity and consistent, coherent values and skills. You live from a set of consistent values that do not zig and zag under outside influences. People experience consistency in your leadership over an extended period of time. Values and skills combine to give people trust in your leadership. Trust is built as you demonstrate consistency in values, skills, and actions.

The importance of trust is apparent. In a context of discontinuous change, response requires risk, experimentation, and travel into uncharted territory. Few will follow you unless they have deep trust that you can give them a context in which their basic necessities and needs will be met along the way. Trust is the invisible bond, or covenant, between the leader and the people that makes the journey possible. This covenant emerges from commitment to the people being led. Once trust is lost, it is extremely difficult to reestablish this broken bond.

In the Book of Hosea, God uses personal and intimate language to describe the relationship that exists with God's people. These people are not just a project. They are "my people." Your covenant with the people in your congregation must mimic the strength of God's covenant. Such a bond of identity, commitment, and love forges a covenant of trust where people come to know that you are for them and with them in your leadership. Like Moses, as a missional leader you lead people into a place that is unpredictable and calls for a high level of adaptability, risk, and courage. They must trust you to follow you in innovating missional change.

Trust operates as a barometer of interpersonal effectiveness. It is not measured in the terms seen in Figure 7.1. Instead, trust operates as an alternative to distrust, as in Figure 7.2.

Figure 7.1. Locating Trust (1).

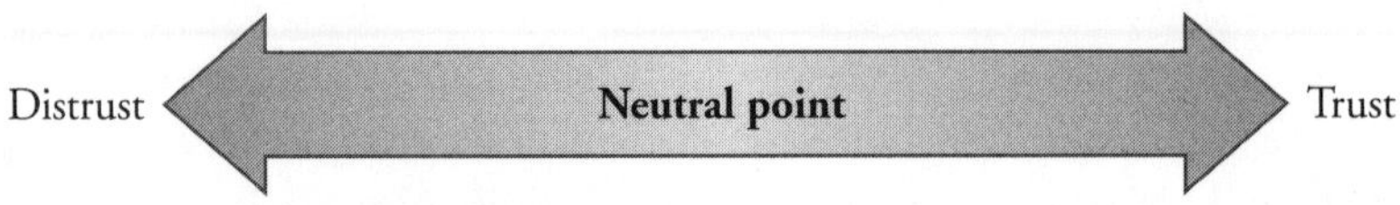

Figure 7.2. Locating Trust (2).

To the extent that people distrust me, whether it is my motives, intentions, theology, capabilities, or what I say, they will protect themselves from my influence. They will be on guard around me, questioning what I do and say because I am the one who said it. Of course, I want people to question and debate what I say, and I want them to discover for themselves whether they believe me. But if people question what I say because of who I am, they can reach only a neutral point in their relationship with me, not a point of trusting me.

One of the pastors we worked with scored low on the trust dimension in our Pastor/Leader instrument. Devastated by the results, she could not believe the low scores. In her distress, she wanted to know how to fix this problem. She wanted a formula that would create immediate trust.

We advised the distraught pastor to enter into a three-to-four-month journey with this issue, and to begin developing awareness of what actions result in people distrusting her. We asked her to meet with twenty or more people and tell them: "I'm beginning to learn that there are some people who distrust me. Please don't rescue me by telling me this isn't true. I believe that I'm totally trustworthy, but obviously I do things, and behave in ways, that result in a perception that I cannot be trusted. I want you—no, I implore you—to think about how I may be doing this. If you have some thoughts right now, I would love to hear them. Please don't be afraid of hurting me. This is really important to me. I ask you to do this with the spirit of wanting to help me be a better person."

We advised her just to listen and hear what people said. As she did so, she identified a list of behaviors she was able to reflect on. She understood what people were telling her. She was then ready to try new actions to get different results. She is now well along on her journey.

Conclusion

This chapter has shown how the leader's character is at the core of the overall skills and capacities required to cultivate missional change in a local church. As the stories of other leaders addressing self-awareness, authenticity, maturity, conflict, and trust indicate, this is not a program for learning useful technical skills. This process is a life journey that considers the basic nature of you are as a leader. As a pastor in Pennsylvania said to us, "This has changed my life. I've learned how to move past technique and program to the really basic and important issues of leadership. It's revolutionized my leadership!" From here, we move on to the next chapter, which develops the essential elements for empowering the people of a congregation in missional life.

CHAPTER 8

Cultivating the People of God for a Missional Future

BILL WAS COMPLETING HIS FIRST YEAR AS PASTOR of a large church in the Pacific Northwest. He moved there after successfully growing a medium-sized congregation in the Southeast. He had a strong reputation as a mature, sensible, solid leader; he was an above-average preacher who spoke his mind and owned the courage to lead people. The congregation had a long history and prided itself on the lengthy tenure of its pastors. Now there was a restless sense of staleness and the need for change beyond bringing in a new leader.

In his early forties, Bill came into the call process with great energy, vigor, and vision. The board and congregation were ready for his energy and thrilled with his sense of command and direction. With Bill, they felt they had found a new lease on life. Within a few months he shared with the board his vision for reaching the growing number of young families moving into the old, established neighborhood around the church. The vision would require planning and change that involved remodeling parts of the church complex, reshaping the two worship services, and taking a new approach to advertising and marketing. Bill detailed a strategy for growth as a series of stages to be phased in over a two-year period. He became more excited and confident as the plans were laid out with the board and discussed with the congregation. It was clear he could communicate with passion, clarity, and energy. He was also an efficient manager who got things done. By this point, he had already aligned the staff with the new vision for growth and hired several new people into family ministry positions.

After a church vote, it looked like a green light to move ahead with the initial phases of the growth strategy, including significant adjustment to the two worship services as well as renovation of some space in the complex. Ten months later, however, almost 20 percent of the members had left the church, and there were undercurrents swirling around, questioning Bill's leadership. People were taking sides, and Bill was painfully confused by the turn of events. He wondered if he should tender his resignation and look for another church.

Bill's story is not unusual. A highly skilled leader with a lot of personal character somehow runs afoul of a congregation even after a vote on the pastor's strategies for change.

Another story may highlight what is happening in Bill's situation. Mark moved to another city to take up a seminary teaching post. With his Japanese American wife, Nina, and their two boys, they joined a Japanese congregation near their home. When Mark and his family arrived, the congregation consisted mainly of aging members with some young families sprinkled among them. Over a period of time, Mark and Nina contributed to the life of the congregation by participating in events and helping with worship services. It was clear, though, that this congregation with such a long history in the community was failing. It had lost touch with any sense of being able to create a different future despite having hope that Mark, as a seminary professor, and his wife, as a professional in business, could assist in turning the church around.

As in Bill's case, the congregation was optimistic that this couple's energy and skills would bring strategies to improve the situation. Mark and Nina, however, took a different approach from Bill's. Instead of presenting a vision and a plan, they began listening to the members' stories. This took time because initially people were reluctant to tell their stories. But after a time, the stories began to emerge. Those stories told of the pathos of the past as well as dreams of the future. Over a period of several years, the people of this congregation rediscovered the stories that had once given them life. Out of these engagements they began to discern experiments that they could attempt in finding renewed hope and energy within themselves. Mark and Nina had not come to these people, as was expected, with a bold vision or a four-year plan. Instead, they came with a commitment to know and love these people where they were and to use their skills to cultivate a new sense of hope and energy.

In our experience, it is common to find leaders like Bill. They have high trust in terms of character and excel in articulating a vision for a desired future. But they often lack the skill and capacity to know how to cultivate and form the people themselves. It seems that people like Bill have been trained to believe if they have the right vision and enough energy, people will follow them. This has been true in the past, but in a time of major change it is no longer the norm. Bill needs to discover what Mark and Nina learned in other settings: the key to innovating new life and mission in a congregation is not so much a strategy for growth as it is cultivation of people themselves. It is from among the people that the energy and vision for missional life emerge.

Leaders enable formation of a missional church to the extent they are able to cultivate this process in others. For too long, church leaders have been obsessed with the search for the program, tactic, or strategic plan that delineates a goal, sets out a path, and aligns people in moving toward and realizing a predetermined future. Behind this obsession lurks the continued belief that leadership is not only about defining and shaping a preferred future but also making such a planned future happen. In this sense, no matter what words are used in regard to serving or nurturing, leadership turns into methods of controlling and manipulating others to achieve predetermined ends. In the end, people are ends to a leader's goals.

Leaders in discontinuous change recognize that they cannot determine or define the future. In an in-between period, we *are* in between. The world we once inhabited as a church is largely gone. Many of the habits and skills needed in the past are less functional today. As we move through this transition, we cannot define or predict what the church will look like down the road. How do you lead in this context? God's future is not in a plan or strategy that you introduce; it is among the people of God. God brings the future toward us. God's future is already being cultivated in the church among the ordinariness of one another.

There are powerful implications for leadership in this. The leader's primary calling is to cultivate a people and nourish the conviction that

God's future is among them. Michelangelo was once observed pushing a huge rock through the streets of Florence. The bemused citizens turned to him in his exertions to ask, "Why are you pushing that mighty rock, Michelangelo?" His response was simple but decisive: "Because there's a person inside longing to get out!"

Leading others is like the great sculptor's task. It is the passionate recognition that God's missional future for the church is present among the people of God. The birth stories of Jesus, the annunciation of Mary, and other scriptural narratives tell us that God's future is among the least expected people—even those in the church we write off as unimportant. The leader's role is to help form a people among whom God's future is called forth. In our experience, this process of formation requires some specific skills focused on the formation of missional people:

1. Fostering a missional imagination among the people themselves
2. Cultivating growth through specific practices and habits of Christian life
3. Enabling people to understand and engage the multiple changes they face in their lives
4. Creating a coalition of interest, dialogue, energy, and experimentation among the people of the congregation

Table 8.1 suggests a contrast between how leaders often view their role and responsibility and seeing the formation of a people as the primary focus for leadership.

Fostering *a* Missional Imagination

Imagination is not a matter of fanciful dreams or irrational, fantastical thinking. Imagination is first of all about the capacity to use forms of thinking other than linear, cause-and-effect, and ordered. It is thinking that is creative, outside the box, intuitive, unexpected according to accepted knowledge or wisdom. Einstein demonstrated this kind of thinking at the beginning of the twentieth century when he imagined that time was not an absolute. Picasso's art invited the possibil-

TABLE 8.1. *Moving Toward a Missional Imagination.*

Common Leadership Thinking	*Leaders Developing a Missional Imagination*
Strategies for attraction and growth of church come from leaders or board with congregational agreement.	Create dialogue and listening among people; within their stories are hints and directions for missional life.
People *come* to church; the building is the center of religious life.	Church is the people engaged in their context in relationship with others.
People receive teaching, preaching, and belonging as religious goods and services.	People are formed in a way of life.
The church is about experts who develop programs to "minister" to specific groups.	The church as a center of formation where people codevelop the skills they need.

ity of seeing the familiar from multiple angles at the same time. When Karl Barth wrote his famous *Romerbrief* at the beginning of the twentieth century, he was painting an imagination about God's word to modern culture that was far outside the boxes previous theologians had built. Stanley Hauerwas and William Willimon did the same thing in 1989 when they wrote their book *Resident Aliens.* Brian McLaren is doing the same with books such as *A New Kind of Christian.* Each is seeking to describe a new imagination that operates in another kind of field in which we can think and act differently as Christians.

We encounter imagination in the biblical texts. Jesus introduces parables and narratives that cause people to see reality from an alternative angle that challenges and upsets their world. The story of the Good Samaritan, for example, challenges people to see relationships, duties, and ethnic divisions in a significantly different way. In that story we see that God is not confined to preconceived ideas about who is and isn't in the kingdom. Jewish listeners must have had difficulty receiving this story because Samaritans were viewed as the most vulgar and deceptive of groups who could never deserve God's care. But here is a Samaritan acting with the character of God. These listeners were being compelled to ask, "If this is what the kingdom is about, then what kind of kingdom is this?" The question is even more urgent when, later on, Jesus tells these people that it will be easier for a camel to go through the eye of a needle than for a rich man to enter the kingdom. Again, the listeners are compelled to ask the same question: "What kind of kingdom is this?" In this way, Jesus' stories and parables create a space where his listeners might develop a new imagination about the kingdom of God.

An important capacity in cultivating missional imagination is to help the congregation see familiar stories and taken-for-granted situations anew. This is what Mark and Nina did in their Japanese American congregation. They asked people to tell stories about the early days of the congregation. The congregation shared stories about their internment as children in World War II. They talked about returning after the war and how they rebuilt community. Younger people in the congregation listened to these stories and wanted to hear more. As they interacted with one another through this storytelling, there emerged a new energy to look at how this congregation, in its community, could return to being a vital place of witness and mission. Again, this is not primarily about strategy and planning but rather a way in which a congregation engages the biblical material and comes to see its own reality from a new angle of meaning.

Imagination also deals with the capacity to entertain what is not yet present but can be encouraged to emerge from the core of one's deepest convictions. Imagination accesses what otherwise would be inaccessible. For example, if in an in-between time the future cannot be planned, strategized, or controlled but is among God's people, then a leader must know how to cultivate missional imagination among people. This is more than getting people to think the right way. If that were the case, then more classes in teaching and better preaching would suffice. Imagination means forming in people the capacity to reconnect with the biblical story in a way that enables them to discern what God is doing among them. This is what is happening in the biblical stories of exile. When the people of God are taken captive from Jerusalem to Babylon, they weep and lament their great loss. What takes place in the strange world of Babylon, however—a place no Jew could ever have imagined living in—is rediscovery of the core stories of Israel and reimagining the meaning of being the people of God.

This painful process was essential for Israel to understand the shape of the future God was forming in them.

In California's Central Valley, this process is always being repeated. Along Highway 99 there are a long string of small towns with congregations that have served their communities well for many generations. These congregations were largely white in composition and formed a way of life congruent with their farming communities. Their way of life is now being challenged by a different population moving into the area. Sandy has been a long-term pastor in one of these towns. His home is just down the street from the church building and the town center. In his backyard plot, Sandy grows some of the tastiest tomatoes anyone could want, as well as apples and other vegetables because in this part of the valley produce grows quickly in the rich soil. But the growth in Sandy's garden is no longer paralleled by growth in his congregation. The nearby Air Force base moves people out of the area, while an increasing number of Mexican Americans are moving into the community. As a result, the people of the congregation are confused. The normal patterns of church growth through birth and new people moving into town to serve at the Air Force base are no longer there. The congregation looks out at a town of new people who worship in a different kind of church with services unlike their own. They feel as though they are in exile in their own community.

Sandy openly admits that this has been a difficult time for the congregation as they come to terms with permanent change. He has not tried to pretend or promise people a new solution that will change everything. Instead, he quietly works with the people, listening to their stories, bringing those stories into conversation with some of the biblical stories we've discussed in this book. Slowly—because it is slow—the people of this congregation are beginning to ask new questions about what God may be doing in their town and how they need to understand themselves in the midst of change. There are no answers here about a people who have quickly emerged with new strategies. They are a people who, in their sense of loss and exile, are learning to ask new questions about their role as God's people in the community.

Leaders cultivate the missional imagination—in the sense of fostering, nurturing, promoting—by listening to and engaging their congregation's collective stories, fears, concerns, and dreams about who they are and where God is leading them. They then connect the people with biblical stories that invite new questions about themselves. This cultivation of imagination takes time because it is a way of life. A leader can expect this change to be a work in progress for a number of years. This does not mean nothing will happen for a while, but listening to people's stories and entering into dialogue around the biblical stories cannot be done in a few short months.

Alan once spent a full year with a group of eight people experimenting in this listening and dialogue before they began to catch on to the conviction that God's future was really among them. This group met every Tuesday night for supper, dialogue, storytelling, and engagement with Scripture. The storytelling addressed some of the ways they were experiencing change. The biblical engagements worked through various stories Jesus told about the kingdom. People in the group agreed to follow some simple practices each day such as taking time for prayer, scripture reading, and a period when they would stop and listen to God and write in their journal. Eight months into this process, some members of the group began connecting with the notion that the dreams and hopes within their own stories pointed to how God was calling them into places of witness and mission they could never have imagined. Over time they discovered that solving a problem does not require a pastor or board coming up with programs, but instead that the resources and answers are within them to shape the congregation's witness and mission.

Alan learned about this kind of cultivation some years earlier. The downtown church he pastored was growing and flourishing. Pastors of other churches wanted him to speak to them about how to achieve similar growth in their congregation. He agreed. At first, he felt awkward and artificial because inside he didn't feel he was doing anything. Since the people of his congregation were driving the creativity and energy of the church, he didn't know what to tell the other pastors. Then he realized he was contributing a great deal to the congregation's creativity and imagination through a number of actions:

- Painting word pictures of the possible meanings of the kingdom in their context
- Creating spaces of permission where people could experiment

- Joining experiments without directing
- Forming groups built around basic Christian practices and rooted in neighborhoods
- Continually showing people how God's imagination is fostered as they enter simple, normal, human relationships with their neighbors free of manipulation and the need to market the Gospel

There were so many examples of how people became a part of that community over the years because they sensed it was a place where their imagination, gifts, and dreams would be welcomed, blessed, and encouraged. There was no five-year plan or three-phase strategy. The plan was to invite people into practices of Christian life, listen to one another's stories, dialogue about the biblical narratives in light of the neighborhood and the changes they were experiencing, and release people into Spirit-shaped experiments. This kind of work cannot be made an addendum to some other strategy. Cultivating the missional imagination of God's people is the core strategy.

Make no mistake, this is not an easy shift in leadership. Whenever we describe this way of leading, the response among pastors young and old is often resistance. Leaders feel that if they tried this kind of leadership in their congregation, they would be fired because people expect a strong leader to offer plans and a firm direction. In such cases, we point out that it would be foolish to simply shift to the kind of leadership we're describing. These leaders need to keep doing what they are doing and at the same time start a few small experiments with people in cultivating a more missional kind of leadership.

But others ask questions that make it clear they cannot begin to believe leaders shouldn't have a strategic plan with phases for growth and a plan for marketing their congregation. These leaders are much more difficult to engage because they have a deep-seated conviction that leadership means clear direction, clear plans, and control of that direction. This worldview remains dominant in our churches. Many leaders relax, however, when they hear of the process we are describing and see that it is not intended to bring wholesale change to a congregation all at once, but to develop small steps and experiments. They grow excited as they realize they can proceed in small stages over a number of years. Leaders come to us in conferences to tell us that this way of leading has given them back their ministry and released them from the huge, harsh burden of having to be a superleader.

This kind of leadership does not cultivate people's imagination for imagination's sake. It moves toward *missional* action. Leaders are inviting and cultivating a people who can rediscover and reconnect with this missional calling as they engage their imagination.

Cultivating Growth

Cultivation is an ancient word taken from gardening and horticulture. A cultivator works with plants in the garden. It is an organic rather than mechanical or tactical metaphor. One who cultivates a garden understands that the life and purpose of each plant is not something over which one has control. Cultivation involves working with the plant in its growth. You provide the right kind of soil. You watch that the right amount of water is present along with sufficient protection from the sun and cold. Leadership as cultivation involves creating the environment in which people's missional imagination can bud and develop among a community. Some of the illustrations that follow are examples of cultivating such a space.

We usually think of growth in terms of (1) personal, inner-directed discipleship; (2) discernment of gifts for use in mission and ministry; or (3) a numeric increase in a congregation's size. But cultivating growth in people goes beyond this standard description. It involves helping people think outside the box currently shaping their understanding of Christian life and the church. In discontinuous change, people are stretched. They want to stop the change and return to stability. Cultivating growth means helping people live in this tension. It introduces new practices for living as Christians that initially seem awkward and disconnected from what they have thought of as normal ways of being Christian.

Cultivating growth requires formation through habits and practices. What are these habits and practices, and how does a leader go about forming them in a people?

This question is in itself a book. Some of the best work in the area of Christian formation for mission was done many years ago by the Church of the Savior in Washington, D.C., under the leadership of

Gordon and Mary Cosby and through the writing of Elizabeth O'Conner, who was a member of that community.[1] Their books would help any leader learn the process of forming a people around practices of missional life. Here we describe some of the basic practices we believe are central to formation of a missional community.

Briefly, a leader develops skills in these practices by becoming part of a group of leaders willing to take the journey of learning these skills for themselves and holding each other accountable. This is the only way the leader can begin to invite people in the congregation to experiment in these practices.

Other practices could be described. The discussion here is not intended to be exhaustive. Worship, or the sacrament of the Lord's Supper, is also a central practice for cultivating a missional environment. The practices discussed here are examples of how leaders might go about shaping a missional environment amid discontinuous change.

The Purpose *of* Practices

The use of practices has a twofold aim. First, we simply need to relearn some of the habits and practices that Christians have developed over the centuries that assist in cultivating Christian identity. These habits of formation have been largely forgotten because we assumed that most people were Christians just by the fact of living in this culture formed as Christians. We now realize it was never quite like that and that we've lost the habits and skills of Christian formation.

Second, the practices help us discern how we are shaped by habits that deform Christian life. The wisdom of the church through the centuries is recognized in that certain practices help us unmask our captivity while forming us in Christian life. Practices cultivate an environment for learning discernment and developing an alternative imagination as God's people. Here are some of these practices.

Daily Offices

Monastic communities were formed around a rhythm of life called the daily offices. At specific times each day, bells rang to call the community from its diverse occupations to gather for a brief period of Scripture reading and prayer. This daily rhythm shaped people in a way of life by reminding them that their life and allegiance belonged to God.

Why is the practice of offices important for missional formation? It creates a context in which two critical things happen. First, one is daily shaped in the imagination that life is a gift from (and belongs to) God. We gain understanding of grace and gift and recognition that we do not make life happen. Rather, life is a gift to be embraced, a vocation to be lived in the presence of God and others. This is the opposite of expressive individuals for whom life is all about getting, gaining, and keeping.

Second, the offices assist us in becoming aware of how easily and incessantly other demands and stories enter our own life, and the community's, recasting us in ways other than the gospel. This is why the New Testament describes the church as a people formed by the cross. It is a journey with a cost. The cross remains at the center of discipleship. In this case it is the continuing recognition of how deeply the narratives of the culture control the way we live. In the practice of the offices, we remind each other of the cost of this journey; we learn to corporately discern how we crowd out the one essential focus for our lives as a people, the Lordship of Christ.

What might use of offices look like in practice? Few people either want or desire to be monastic. We work hard in our vocations and have extreme demands placed upon every aspect of our lives. We are saturated selves with so many conflicting demands that we become not a single person but many selves who appear and disappear according to the place and role demanded of us.[2] This is not an argument for withdrawing from our worlds into separated, monasterylike gatherings. That is an option for some, but the offices described here are for discipleship formation in a congregation.

One group of church leaders began this at the staff level. Several staff members became aware of how their lives were so shaped by the busyness of multiple demands that they could rarely practice the disciplines of listening and discernment. They agreed to an experiment to commit themselves to a period in which they would practice stopping the work of the congregation at designated points during the day and give time briefly to Scripture and prayer.[3] The book they used is organized around the seven days of the week, each focusing on a central element of Christian life (resurrection, creation, incarnation, Spirit, community, and cross). Each day is divided into four short sets of liturgy built around Scripture reading and prayer. The commitment involved keeping two of these offices each day. They did not need to be together to do so. Wherever they found themselves, at the agreed time, they would practice the office. At first, it was an energizing adventure. They felt keenly in touch with something that gave shape and meaning to life.

But within a few brief months something else began happening. The times of office keeping would pass and they would realize that the events of the day had so shaped their time that the office was neglected. It became difficult to keep this simple practice. Here is where discernment can begin. This simple, corporate practice helped them articulate how hard it is in our culture to shape life around an alternative story. Incarnating that commitment into actual practices is quite challenging.

This awareness engendered a process of asking questions about the mechanisms that shape life and give it determinative meaning. Why are we so deeply embedded in a context where busyness and all the demands of a day drive us such that we feel like the proverbial rat running on a treadmill? We live in a culture where an increasing number of people in our congregations feel incredibly insecure about their future and are aware of how many hours they must work. Technology means we are not *less* busy; instead, our work is now a twenty-four, seven reality.

Where are the places we can be formed by an alternative story? Is there another rhythm of life that is a counterstory to this dominant narrative? What do we do when we realize that despite our greatest longing our lives are driven by narratives that contradict the future Jesus called into being? The practice of keeping daily office is a subversive activity in this culture. It confronts these questions. But the intention is not to induce guilt. If that is the result, then one is not grasping the nature of grace or the purpose of the offices. Only as we enter and struggle with the offices do we discover the challenge of the journey that faces us in shaping ecclesial communities in America.

Practicing Hospitality

Hospitality is an ancient church practice whose purpose has been largely forgotten. Cultivating a missional environment involves recovery of this practice. Hospitality is not an evangelism strategy but a genuine and complete welcoming of the stranger,[4] involving all that it meant in ancient Middle Eastern cultures. Today, the stranger can easily be the person next door, the widow whose children live far away, or many of the young people who crave conversation and acceptance from an older generation. In a culture as isolating and fragmenting as our own, people are strangers to one another.

Hospitality, a profoundly Christian habit, is an alternative practice in a culture where people feel like strangers to one another even in their own neighborhood. Our antennae are attuned to the fact that almost every situation in which we find ourselves has attached to it some means of using us as a commodity. How many of us are familiar with the endless stream of surveys assaulting us wherever we go? In a shopping mall, over the telephone, passing through an airport, well-dressed men and women want us to stop and answer a few questions about one thing or another. These are methodologies for discovering people's likes and dislikes. We are used as objects and commodities to improve a service that will sell. Such experiences raise our guard against almost everyone who is a stranger. No wonder we are hesitant to welcome the stranger, who in our culture is viewed as a threat or danger. Modernity was birthed in suspicion, and we are socialized to be wary of everyone outside a small circle of people.

The Neighborhood Watch program is an example of what has happened to people in the urban and suburban neighborhoods of North America. When you see a sign that says "This is a Neighborhood Watch community," you know that the people who live there do not know one another. To protect goods and children from the stranger, these "neighbors" must now create a program to wall off the outsider because the person is dangerous. Schools create regulations to ensure that no adult can enter this public, social space without passing through a well-monitored world of secretaries and cameras. Grandparents and friends are not allowed to pick up children after school without the express written consent of the parent who presents a permission form in writing to the school; a phone call is not sufficient.

People no longer know one another in our society.[5] We create more ways to safeguard ourselves from the stranger while our lives keep fragmenting. The gospel invites Christians into a different way of life that addresses fear and suspicion of the stranger. People hunger to be welcomed today. There is a deep longing to be recognized and given worth in a culture moving in the opposite direction. Welcoming the stranger is a revolutionary activity in forming a parallel culture. The Bible speaks of a day when there will no longer be strangers. The imagery of the consummation of God's salvation is of a great banquet. God welcomes the stranger. "All who were not my people" (1 Peter) are invited to the great banquet table of life. Jesus speaks in parables of the great feast resulting from his entering the world. His disciples are urged to go out into the world and invite the strangers, those who do not fit into the normal structure of the culture and who are viewed with suspicion, and invite them to the banquet.

What is disarming about these images is the absence of an agenda to make people into something. Hospitality is a way of practicing the eschatological future by welcoming the stranger to our table as honored guests. In the biblical stories, God uses the stranger to introduce the strangeness of truth to a community of faith. To remain aloof from the stranger, to be fearful of the stranger by building a wall of protection against such people (as we see happening with gated communities today) is to build a wall against the possibility of encountering the disturbing reality of God's truth.

A missional environment is formed by the practice of hospitality. Members set aside an evening a month to welcome the stranger into their homes. The stranger may be a neighbor or someone within their circle of acquaintance. It is important that they invite someone to their table other than a friend or church member. This may be a neighbor, work associate, or acquaintance from a coffee shop or the children's sports team. Fear of the stranger is so high in this culture that inviting someone far outside the circle of acquaintance is too great a first step. The purpose of such invitation is to treat the stranger as a guest, to experience the gracious table of God.

Why is hospitality such an important practice? It requires one to stop a busy, demanding routine for a period of time and focus attention on the stranger for the sake of the stranger. We quickly discover how this simple act of faithfulness and witness is experienced as interference. It is an act that forces us to confront how our lives are driven by agenda and by demands that push away any relational encounter with another.

Creating a gracious table does not have an agenda to convert the stranger but instead to create space to listen—nothing more. Hospitality is best expressed in the unspoken code of Middle Eastern people as to a stranger coming to their door. If a visitor comes to your door, feed the person; rest and care for the visitor; only after three days do you ask him or her what he or she wants. What a gift that would be to give people today. Such practice would be a transformative action in the suburban neighborhood of most congregations.

As hospitality develops in the congregation and people come together in small group meetings, part of the conversation can be shaped around what people experience when welcoming the stranger. In the initial months, they may find that it is an imposition on their busy lives. This is the natural process of awakening to our own captivity, the cultural lies about what is important and essential. In a strange way, welcoming the stranger begins our own conversion to the gospel of the kingdom.

In the end, what is welcoming the stranger about? In the New Testament there is the inspiring story of Jesus coming to meet two distraught disciples following his crucifixion. They are on a road, returning home to their former lives. They are bereft of hope because their world has fallen apart with the execution of Jesus. The stranger meets them on their journey and walks with them. They cannot believe that, as they hear from the stranger, someone could not know of recent events. In their own grief they have no perspective as to who the stranger walking with them is. Even though he speaks of hope and expectation, and the promises of the Scriptures, the disciples still have no idea who is walking with them. Then, as night is falling, they extend the natural invitation to the stranger to eat with them. At the table, sitting beside each other in this place of sharing, the stranger breaks bread and their eyes are suddenly opened to the truth of who is sitting with them. The true identity of the stranger becomes visible only at the table and in the elements of eating together.

The truth about the people in our neighborhood, community, and culture is experienced in relationship around the table. The truth about the creation of a new kind of culture is experienced in the practice of hospitality.

The Practice of Learning

Congregations are increasingly composed of people with little sense of the Christian story. It is crucial to form a learning community. After a sermon, a man who has attended church for almost three years tells a friend that it was one of the most helpful sermons he's ever heard. When asked why, he says he never knew that the book of Acts was written when Paul was no longer alive. Though this event might be considered insignificant, it indicates the loss of any coherent sense of the Biblical story.

The congregation today must become a learning center. In Washington, D.C., the Church of the Savior has practiced this way of life with its members for years. Known as the School for Christian Living and the Servant Leadership School, it invites people into a process of lifelong engagement in learning. The school incarnates the kind of missional learning practice needed to shape every church on this continent.

These Christian practices are not intended to add a new burden or another set of religious rules but to create an environment in which people might be formed. They are practical ways of living out the implications of Romans 12: the transformation of the whole self toward God's kingdom. Such practices, however, take time to develop. People should be invited into them as partners in a learning process that requires time and patience. The spiritual resources for forming a missional church are rooted in this form of relationship.

Enabling Change

As we've discussed earlier in the book, most congregations are facing discontinuous, challenging, and unpredictable change. It's not a matter of small adjustments in a stable system. We are in a period that makes it impossible to have much clarity about the future and how it is going to be shaped. Therefore those leaders who believe they can address the kind of change we are facing by simply defining a future that people want, and then setting plans to achieve it, are not innovating a missional congregation. They are only finding new ways of preventing a congregation from facing the discontinuous change it confronts.

Effective change leadership is like the process of creating a good marriage. Healthy, strong marriages are a combination of two personalities who work diligently at the points of conflict, difference, and change that inevitably confront the relationship. They choose to enter and move through the difficult issues and hard work. In so doing, they became something more than two separate people. A strong, healthy marriage emerges from willingness to travel in and through the hard work of change, rather than avoiding it. In a similar manner, as an effective missional leader you need to understand the processes of change amid discontinuity. You must recognize the difference between change and transition. Change is ceaselessly happening to us; since it comes from the outside, we usually have no control over it.

Tim called Alan one day, upset and furious because the senior pastor of his church had said a program Tim had developed and grown as a volunteer staff person would be discontinued. The evening before, the official board had decided the program would end in a few weeks. Tim's anger was not primarily directed toward the decision about terminating the program. He said he could deal with that because he understood that some cuts and decisions were to be made in programs. His frustration was at the failure to really process these decisions with the people involved. The pastor was acting as if the decisions were his to make and everyone else had to fall in line.

Tim's response is a key indicator of what we call *transition.* Tim is responding internally to the external change and how it was handled. Good missional leadership knows how to manage both change and transition. Alan encountered a similar situation when the staff of a large church asked him to work with them on critical change issues. The staff described everything they had done, including extensive communication to bring the church members along with them. They were concerned about people's resistance to what was happening. One lay leader of the church took Alan aside and said: "We've been through a lot of change, all right. But it's all been top-down. We've been told what the changes will be and how we ought to support them. There's been lots of communication, but it's all been in announcements, letters, and glossy images telling us about what has already been decided. Some of us are up to here with change, and we're really angry!"

Alan shared this story with the leadership. They were surprised and hurt by this comment from key lay leadership in the church. After the initial shock, the associate pastor paused and said, "You know, they're right! This is exactly what we've done. I think we've blown it!" The others then found courage to talk. One staff member explained how she had sensed this was the problem but didn't know how to raise it among other staff who seemed so pumped and excited about all the plans they were developing. The senior pastor, after listening to the conversation for a while, asked the rest what should be done. The staff realized what had happened and called together the lay leadership. At that meeting, they acknowledged the criticism and apologized to these leaders for their actions. The entire tone of the group shifted. There was a sense of relief from the lay leaders, and with it emerged laughter and lightness. In this new atmosphere, the staff discovered empowerment in inviting the lay leaders on a journey of change.

Internal emotional responses are crucial for a congregation caught up in change. The transition determines how we react to or engage with the changes we face. In leadership it is not the changes that get to you but the transitions. All of us have a real, inner emotional response to change that is based in rational evaluation but goes deeply into who we are and how we've been shaped. This is why change requires time and why it is important to pay attention to what is happening inside people undergoing change. This does not mean leaders give up on leading change; it means they have to develop the skill of paying attention to people's emotional responses.

One group of lay leaders visited a large church that was running a leadership summit on how to reach the unchurched. They were told that large foyers were now as important as (if not more important than) the worship space. One lay leader, an architect, became excited about creating a welcoming space for new people. By the time the group returned, he had developed a wonderful design. At their church, they met as a board and talked about the idea of redesigning the foyer, which would require using some of the worship space. Everyone was still excited about the proposal. The architect was asked to present the idea to the church at the next meeting.

As he shared his big idea (with the enthusiasm of someone who wanted to reach others for the Gospel), tension began rising in the room. One could feel people's awkwardness and uneasiness even before the presentation ended. As soon as the architect leader sat down, people were on their feet. A creative, forward-thinking person who ordinarily loved new ideas and risk blurted out, "How could you think of doing such a thing?! I've been in this church for ten years and dreamt of the day when I could walk my daughter down this aisle at her wedding day, and now you want to ruin my church!" This was not a rational response; it was an emotional response from someone caught in transition.

Most leaders who introduce change into a congregation have little sense of how to address the transition. This is why so many change strategies fail. A leader who wants to innovate missional change must learn to deal with change and transition. In the case of the architect and his redesign, the leadership team was wise. As soon as they heard these responses from creative people, they knew there were other issues. They quickly pulled the idea off the table. The architect had difficulty with this because he was already talking to people about potential next steps in building design. But the team came together to ask what had happened. They evaluated their actions to understand what was happening in the congregation. They took the distinction between change and transition seriously and discussed what had occurred at the meeting using those concepts as a framework.

They immediately realized what was happening. The next step was to talk with one another about how they might address the transition issues. The amazing part of the conversation is that others on the team talked about their own transition experiences. They too felt like the man who wanted to walk his daughter down the aisle at her wedding. The group discovered they needed to back away from simply making announcements and asking for votes on a change. Instead, they needed to paint pictures and share stories of where they were and what they were dreaming about, and then invite people into conversation and dialogue in all kinds of ways.

As the leadership team did this, they came together and shared what they were hearing in dialogue. They learned that people were not opposed to dreaming and thinking outside the box about new approaches to reaching their community. The congregation members, however, needed time to process their own inner feelings. This didn't include ideas brought from the outside and imposed on them. When given the chance to dialogue and talk they could come up with their own imaginative ideas about how to become a more welcoming people. In the end, the leadership's dream of the new jazzy atrium with a latte bar and seats never materialized. Instead, a new spirit emerged in the congregation as it took on the dream of creating a welcoming environment for others.

Creating Coalition

If leaders are not supposed to develop some grand plan or strategy that leads the congregation toward a predefined or preferred future, what are they supposed to do as their people navigate the in-between time when it is not possible to discern how God's intended future will unfold? The answer is that, besides fostering missional imagination and encouraging growth, leadership involves empowerment, mentoring, and equipping coalitions of people. *Coalition,* taken from the Latin verb "to grow together," is not a power group advocating issues or positions; nor is it necessarily the traditional small group meeting every week for Bible study, prayer, and mutual support. As a church wrestles with questions about its role, mission, and engagement with changing neighborhoods, work patterns, groups, and issues, one of the leader's roles is to create a space and place where people can talk to each other about such concerns. This is done through introducing practices such as those described previously in this chapter. Sometimes, the leader learns from conversation that numerous people in the church are thinking in similar ways about how they might engage their community. In one church, Alan pastored several people thinking about using the church building to cook a Thursday night meal for the poor in the community. As he heard these conversations, he connected the people. Others heard about the idea, and soon a coalition was meeting to think about how to actually do it. They were not a committee of the church or a traditional small group but a coalition of people with ideas, though not as yet a clear sense of how to move forward. The wonderful thing was that these people would never have found each other, or come together out of affinity, or just been part of a regular small group. They all differed significantly from one another.

The coalition pulled off the Thursday night dinner. As it progressed, it filled up with many people from the community, both well off and poor, sitting at small tables of about six each, eating a meal together (hospitality) and listening to each other's stories. As the dinners continued for several months, Alan heard conversations among congregation members about other ideas from people who had no connection with one another.

One of these conversations was about the fact that feeding poor people (especially single, older males on welfare) just wasn't enough.

But what else could the church do? He brought these people together and helped them form another coalition around this point. Within a month, the new coalition discovered people among them who had gifts that, when put together, fostered a whole new imagination for serving the poor in the community. This coalition worked with government agencies to buy halfway houses in the community for these older men and develop ways to empower their lives. A number of those men gradually became part of the regular small-group life of the church.

These examples of coalition are not formal church committees or traditional small groups. Alan was practicing many of the principles outlined in this book and, while doing so, keeping his discerning eyes and ears open to the conversation the Spirit was cultivating among people. He then connected and introduced people and encouraged them to explore their conversation together to see what the Spirit might be calling forth. This is how coalition can birth mission. Not every coalition, though, does so. Some of them just become regular support groups. But some do fly in new ways and allow mission to be born through the people and by the Spirit.

Each of the factors presented in this chapter describes and illustrates how leaders focus their energy and skill development on forming people. Here the skills are not connected with managing the organization or fitting people into the boxes of church work that needs to be done. They are skills of opening, shaping, and releasing the imagination of people themselves.

CHAPTER 9

Forming a Missional Environment and Culture

SOUTHSIDE COMMUNITY CHURCH IN VANCOUVER, British Columbia, is an example of a church that has worked hard at forming a missional environment and culture. It has self-consciously formed a single church comprising a growing number of congregations built around missional groups and located in specific communities and neighborhoods in the greater Vancouver area.

The church has formed itself in this way to develop small congregations that are incarnationally present in neighborhoods. In their planning and imagination, no one in their larger church community will drive more than a few miles on a Sunday morning or Saturday night because they worship in the community where they live. They then have an overall leadership team that serves these congregations so that each of them receives the best resources of the whole church for its local mission. Southside has even gone so far as to have a common budget among all the congregations so that the resources of the whole are available to each local congregation. This is a wonderful example of leaders with a missional imagination forming a church culture around local, neighborhood mission.

Southside has deliberately shaped its life around living in and being a part of each neighborhood in which a congregation is involved. Thus if you are part of that church you worship in the congregation closest to where you live and commit to investing in the lives of the people in your neighborhood. Some wonderful Christians turn up at that church and don't stay because they aren't willing to make this kind of commitment. The congregations of Southside have a character very much like the people and communities in which they are located. If you attend another congregation that is outside the community in which you live, you quickly feel like a stranger. In fact, the message you pick up is that you really don't belong there, but the leadership will help you connect with the congregation in your community if you want to make the kind of commitment that forms them Southside. This is an example of forming a missional environment. Missional leaders form the overall life of the church as a missional system.

This requires skill in forming an overall structure and organization across the church. Southside has done this incredibly well and is seeing people in the congregational neighborhoods come to Christ and be effectively discipled through the training program.

The Example *of* Southside

Southside illustrates the importance of forming a missional culture. However, the challenge then becomes knowing how to effectively bring new people into that imagination without losing the core commitments and values of the church. Southside has had to wrestle with this issue a great deal as new people often don't understand the ethos (culture of the church) or want to change it to meet their personal needs. Southside manages this integration through training in practices and the continuous communication of a mission-shaped theology. We examine the processes of forming a missional culture under four headings:

- Member integration
- Missional culture
- Missional practices
- Missional theology

Member Integration

At Southside, the leaders have set up clear processes whereby everyone coming into the congregations understands what the whole church is about and how he or she can effectively participate. The congregations have also created many points of conversation where those who are full participants can communicate with the leadership and others about what is happening in each congregation and the overall church. They work hard at integration. Without this key work the missional nature of the church, and its focus on being with and among the people of the neighborhood in which they live, would falter and other agendas would take over.

Decisions and actions made in one area of the church's life, especially if it is composed of numerous neighborhood congregations, have implications and consequences for the whole church that can't be predicted. Therefore it becomes important to continuously teach, train, and communicate the values and commitments of the whole church, and then invite people to live into this commitment in their context. This is how the church leads and manages the complexity of its mission-shaped structure. Leaders must always work with the interdependent nature of all interaction among the various congregations. Once a month a large celebration event is planned at which each congregational community presents its activities and how God is engaging the members in their neighborhood. The overall leadership shares in some way the overall vision of the church, and all participate in celebrating what God is doing across the church. Each congregation has a leader who carries the vision of the whole. The congregations are fashioned around mission groups (not the classic small groups) wherein each member relates personal engagement in the neighborhood or workplace for the sake of the kingdom. At every level the church works to integrate people around its common vision, commitments, and values.

Missional Culture

Every congregation has a culture of common habits, beliefs, values, and practices. Southside has put them in writing. A core value is stated as "incarnational living," which determines how it works and sees itself. Culture is a way of life. It is more than any single individual or an aggregate of individuals doing similar things. Southside's way of life encompasses small congregations in neighborhoods and mission groups that intentionally connect with, care for, and share the gospel with people in the neighborhood.

Developing a missional culture is neither simple nor painless. Southside has been working at this for more than ten years and still people join the church, move through its integration process, and nevertheless want to change the culture of the church back to that of an attractional church focused on the needs of its members. It takes a lot of energy and commitment to hold to the vision and maintain the culture. Culture is like a beautiful garden that has to be worked on all the time.

Our experience with the change model is that when a church finds itself predominantly in the performative zone, the place to start is some quiet experiments working with certain aspects of the church, perhaps with mission groups built around practicing hospitality to a specific area or neighborhood. By starting with a small experiment, the leadership has a chance to see something at work that can't be imagined. This enables leaders to envision how other such experiments can be initiated. Gradually, this process encourages the congregation to talk about risking and imagine a new way of being church. The culture starts to change from within the experiments and the invitation to others to join with them.

Missional Practices

In effect, we have already discussed this readiness factor. Spiritual formation refers to those specific habits and values that shape the identity of God's people and forms them in their Christian life as a community. In the long, stable period of North American Christian life, the culture of the country and the churches became almost identical. Christian culture was the guarantor of North American culture. Christian formation was identified with nation and state. The result was overall loss of those practices and habits that make Christians the "peculiar people" and "holy nation" described in 1 Peter. In the post-Christendom period in which we now find ourselves, a growing number of North Americans have little memory of the Christian story and less sense of how Christian formation occurs. One of the most critical leadership issues for the innovation of a missional church is the capacity to form communities of God's people around practices of Christian life. The core of missional leadership lies in the capacity to form community around the kind of practice suggested in the preceding chapter.

Missional practices and formation are not a matter of learning new skills, but rather recovering ways of life that once were at the heart of Christianity. Chris, whom we met in an earlier chapter, has over a three-year period built his staff meetings around the learning of such practices. He has also taken his elders on retreats where they discuss the role and place of practices and then learned to develop some among themselves. This has not resulted in a new churchwide program of Christian practices but is creating an environment in which others ask how they can develop these practices for themselves. Southside is built on a set of practices the mission groups use to define their activities. These practices are not forced on people. Rather, people are invited to experiment and test so they can discover what the practices are all about.

Cultivating missional practice takes time. Practices are largely alien to most pastors, who in modernity were trained in the techniques of counseling, not spiritual formation and religious practice. Leaders themselves need to be grounded in such practices in order to lead others. The congregation has ceased to be a gathering of a covenant community. Modernity has transformed it into a voluntary association of free individuals who join out of need and stay out of personal choice as long as needs are met.

Because missional practices question these core assumptions, those who currently populate congregations strongly resist them. The obstacles residing with both pastors and the people cannot be overestimated. Missional formation is a long process that can't be achieved overnight. But our experience, and that of leaders we have discussed here, is that people become energized and excited when they are invited on this kind of journey. Today, in cities and towns across the continent, all kinds of groups are springing up from the ground of various kinds of Christian practices. Leaders are discovering that a lot of people are ready for this kind of journey.

Missional Theology

We have insisted on the importance of biblical narratives for the formation and functioning of a missional community. The community must live in continuous engagement with the narratives as it addresses, convicts, and converts God's people as missional agents in their specific cultural context. This requires leaders who function as local theologians. The work of theological reflection in a profoundly changing culture must be reintroduced into the daily practices of pastoral life. Theology is not an abstract discipline for the elite with little connection or value for the practical work of congregational leadership. Our time demands leaders who think theologically and help God's people see their world and their struggle in terms of God's encounter with them in Scripture, through history and into the future.

Theological imagination is essential for a leader wanting to form a missional congregation. Mark, for example, who is leading a house church group, reflects on what it means to be God's people in their community. He understands the ideas of God's kingdom and has read several books on missional church. However, as he reads more and works with Scripture, he begins to sense that in the biblical narratives there is this sense of being incarnational, literally being among people. He read Lesslie Newbigin's works and has seen the same message. It dawns on Mark that all he is doing is going to a lot of busy church meetings, driving his young family to church, and missing the people of his neighborhood. This realization births another idea: What if the church is not about attracting people into a building but living as God's people in the public space of their own community and neighborhood? This imagination was birthed out of a willingness to be theologically informed and ask difficult questions about what God might be doing in the neighborhood in the Scriptures. The results are another story, but we can say that an amazing set of engagements has emerged with the community that is transforming the imagination of non-Christians as to the nature of the Gospel.

Engaging *the* Context *of the* Local Church

The next chapter turns to the context in which a local church is rooted. How does a local church learn to listen to and enter its community? This question is addressed in terms of the skills and competencies a leader requires for cultivating missional engagement.

CHAPTER 10

Engaging Context with a Christian Imagination

When Southside Church in Vancouver (which we introduced in the preceding chapter) began about ten years ago, it settled into a struggling community with a large low-income population and difficult social issues. There were fairly simple reasons for settling on this location. There was a vacated church building in the center of the community, and the core team that was initiating this dream lived close by. They decided to live into their convictions on the nature of a missional church and seek to flourish where they found themselves planted.

The challenge they faced was to take the community seriously rather than bring in a preplanned strategy to create a generic church. The leaders decided they would give time to connecting with the various groups in the community. They did so by putting on overalls and beginning to rehabilitate the building into a community center and a worship environment that welcomed people. They visited apartment buildings, schools, and coffee shops, where they met a growing number of people in the community.

One theme that emerged from these growing connections was that this community had no real identity, no points of connection or gathering. As the conversations grew, others were joining Southside, learning the story and choosing to move into the area. An idea began to form among the leadership. The church would create a context of celebration and gathering for this dispersed community of mostly welfare recipients who often felt powerless and quickly moved on to other areas. Rather than developing "come to us" church programs in their building, they imagined creating an annual street festival for and with the community.

What came about was called the Great Big Pig Gig, a street festival sponsored by Southside. One street beside the church building was closed for the day. A huge spit was set up in the middle, and a whole pig was barbecued. Further down the street, a children's play area was created with games and activities. As the smell of the roasting pig moved through the community, people came out of their tiny homes and apartments to see what was happening. Conversations began and relationships were kindled that would last throughout the year.

That was more than ten years ago; the community now looks forward to and helps plan the Pig Gig. They know about Southside as the church that stayed, built community, created programs in the schools, and formed relationships. The story doesn't end there. Now the community is changing again. Other people are moving in, and Southside is asking again what it means to be incarnational in the community. More than this, however, they have learned to create congregations in other areas and neighborhoods of the city, where they listen and seek to create fresh engagement with the people who live there.

Mike, one of the early leaders of Southside, has moved to another part of Vancouver, called South Surrey, where he and a congregation of some eighty people have settled in among the people of this difficult area. Mike used to run a market garden business that he let go in order to join Southside. Talking with Mike or others in the congregation, one notes a common set of values and commitment. They live in the neighborhood and love the people around them. The people in the area are not an object of a church growth strategy; they are deeply loved. Mike will tell you as often as you want to listen, "I love these people." Then he will tell you a story of someone in the community he and others have been loving—a specific person and how that person's life is being changed. For Southside, a neighborhood is not about a demographic profile. The congregation members live in and with and among the people and the community as they find it. So significant is their presence that school principals invite them into their schools and people open their apartments to the folk from Southside.

The contexts in which congregations live are changing. There are fewer and fewer communities with a wholly similar ethnic or racial background. Globalization creates a pluralist culture in which people next door are from around the world. At the same time, technology brings the other side of the world into our living room and workplace. Whether across the street or around the world, church members live in a context of rapid change formed less and less by any kind of Christian imagination.

Denominations spawned local churches that embodied what we might call the "trading area" concept of a retail store. The people who attended a church lived within walking distance. Whether it was a radius of a mile or ten miles, the members of a church lived near the church. This concept changed dramatically in the second half of the twentieth century. The automobile, the 'burbs, the mobile lifestyle of people have rendered this an unworkable concept of the local church today. Now, people regularly drive ten, twenty, or thirty miles to attend a church. In the suburbs, a large church built in an area of little or no population is likely to be filled with commuters. They go to church to receive religious goods and services, but any concept of a local church being geographically based seems no longer meaningful.

Given these factors, how do we define the context of the church? How do we define community? We believe that there is still a place for the local. In fact, it is becoming a much more important factor again as people struggle to find community and a sense of belonging in a world that keeps breaking them apart in the name of mobility, success, and affluence. We believe that churches today are made up of a number of "potential" local communities. Churches like Southside have grasped this idea.

For example, one church we worked with discovered that its members and newcomers came from all over the city. It still wanted to emphasize being a local church for the community that existed around the building. But this intention excluded the majority who drove in from other areas. The church began to develop a new imagination about itself and its locations within the city. Instead of struggling to get everyone to focus on the changing neighborhood around the building (the attractional model of a church focused around a building and its neighborhood) we talked about seeing the church itself as something like an ancient cathedral. It could be the training and equipping center of a number of mission communities rooted in the neighborhoods of its members. This imagination transformed the thinking of the church. The notion of becoming like a cathedral that trained and formed people in their neighborhood, rather than a shopping mall that sucked everything into its vortex, revolutionized how they saw the communities and contexts of their city. A church may therefore have ten, fifteen, or more such local communities in which members can engage.

What are some of the leadership skills required to cultivate churches with this kind of imagination? Though there are many, our experience has shown a number that are critical to this process. Using Southside as an example, we can report that the leaders of this multi-congregation church up in British Columbia spent a lot of time seeking to understand the nature of the changes that were transforming Canada into a secular, pluralist nation. They then sought to understand how these forces of change were being experienced particularly in greater Vancouver, one of the most multicultural cities on the continent, where only 7 percent of the population are part of any church. The leaders then began working at inviting congregations to engage with the people of their neighborhood. The local congregations and mission groups became the key to this process. At the same time, they recognized that these communities were going to keep changing, so they had to learn to think ahead and imagine other futures. In all this, they had to frame continuous change and mission firmly within the context of the biblical story so people could make sense of how their congregation was being defined. Let's look at these leadership activities and skills to more fully understand them.

Increased Understanding *of* Our Society

It is critical to help people grapple with and understand their society. Engaging in a discussion about the changes that affect both society and church is difficult while we're in the middle of it all. Every day, newspapers and other news media determine our thinking in ways we do not begin to understand. Popular articles about the Internet, sexual mores, drugs, high school crime, and similar topics influence our views and responses to change. At this point we don't yet understand enough about the nature, scope, impact, and permanency of the changes. For example, it's unlikely we will live in a drug-free society within the lifetime of our children. So how do we understand the impact of drugs upon our culture, our neighbors, our children, and our workplace in terms of the church? It is not adequate to take a self-righteous view and ignore the realities of our society.

The role of a missional leader is translation, helping people see that "this is that." Leaders can shape an environment that increases people's understanding of the social and cultural forces affecting their lives. Such understanding occurs as people learn two kinds of interconnected skills. The first is discovering how to read their context, to see beneath the surface of supposed facts and distracting events to deeper levels of meaning. To do this, people need to learn to ask new questions of their context and the church.

After working with a large church school class one Sunday morning in Dallas, a large man in his midfifties lumbered up to Alan with questioning eyes. He stated his case quickly and bluntly:

> I've seen lots of change in my life. I'm a Vietnam Vet and have been a police officer for more than thirty years in this city. From where I sit I think one of the biggest problems in our culture today is a lack of commitment on the part of young people. When I joined the police force as a young man all the guys were the same, were trained together, worked together and saw ourselves as part of the same group. But today, I see the new recruits and they don't do it that way anymore. It's just a job and they want to go home and be with their families and have days off. The commitment is just not there anymore. The really important stuff has gone away.

Alan could hear this police officer's confusion and frustration as a Christian in a large church facing big changes. Alan was able to take the time to suggest another picture and then ask a different set of questions about why young adults today might not have the commitment of a previous generation. He talked about Peter Jennings, who had just died, and the great generation of World War II men whom Jennings wrote about. Alan told a couple of stories about young adults he knew. He used those stories to point toward a contrasting picture. The important part of this story is that he was able to make connection in terms of what was happening in the culture, to create new questions in the mind of the confused man before him.

The other important skill is empowering people by way of letting the biblical narratives ask their own questions of our social context. One practice we work with in all our meetings is spending time at the beginning and end of the event dwelling in Scripture. The passage we always use is Luke 10:1–12, which is an account of Jesus sending out the seventy-two ahead of him. On one meeting occasion in southern Georgia, a member of a denominational board raised the question of evangelism and when we were going to tell people about the Gospel. We returned to the Luke passage and talked about why we would keep reading Luke 10 whenever we met but not move on to other texts. This gave us the chance to talk about spending time in Scripture and letting the text get inside of us rather than using Scripture as proof of what we want to say or do.

The discussion was wonderful, and people started to get this idea of dwelling in Scripture before plunging into a meeting, in order to hear God. It was at this point that we turned to the individual who asked the evangelism question and put our own questions to the group. On the basis of Luke 10, what is the "Gospel," and where is the church? The conversations were suddenly transformed as these leaders began to see that the Gospel might not be such a simple package as they thought. The exchange became even more energized as they started to talk about the fact that in this passage the church was being welcomed and given hospitality in towns and villages. The seventy-two were being welcomed as guests in residents' homes, sitting around their table and probably listening to their stories. The whole conversation about evangelism changed as these leaders asked one another, "How do we do that among our churches?" It's a great question for engaging a community; it beats all the abstract demographic profiles these attendees had been using.

Understanding context is a dual process in which you lead people at all levels of the congregation's life into reading their context from a new perspective and give them the tools (such as the simple Luke 10 conversation) that allow the Bible to address them. This kind of leadership is not limited to formal times of teaching or preaching. It happens most effectively as the congregation learns the skills of listening and informal dialogue about context.

Pastors need to gain deeper understanding of our society before they can develop the skills to take society into account in creating a church environment that will generate a missional engagement with society. This requires reading, watching, attending societal group meetings, discussion with others, and intellectual struggle. Understanding does not come easily. It takes place over time and is a result of interaction with others. Staying close to what is taking place within our society has never been more important to pastors.

Church Member Engagement

The big church in a metropolis prided itself on its community involvement. Members gave a lot of money to various needy missions in the city and sent many of their people on short-term mission trips. They even hired an "ethnic" pastor to minister to the multicultural communities moving into the area (though that was not going as well as they had hoped). As the community changed, more and more people in the church were leaving and heading for the new, seeker-focused churches springing up in the expanding suburbs. The senior pastor suggested that instead of opening the doors of the church building to those school children in the community who needed supplies for the coming year, teams of church members could go out to the school. They would meet the kids and their parents, give out supplies, and then stay to help teachers in any way they could.

At first there was tension and resistance to this course of action. Church members asked the obvious question, "Why can't they come to us, like we've always done it in the past?" The pastor and staff persisted in talking to members about the changing community and suggesting how they could get involved. Finally, they set things in motion by heading for the schools.

Twenty teams signed on. Now a whole new set of relationships and connections is developing between the church and its changing community. Members are learning how to engage with people in the community, but outside the usual bounds of designing a way to get those people to come into the building. As a result, this community, this church is now seen as men and women who deeply care for the neighborhood and schools where they live. There have been other results, notably development of an art gallery in the neighborhood and a dance school teaching ballet to children in the area. The pastor and the church community see all this as an opportunity to serve. Members of the church are involved in developing a coffee house, serving people as guests and developing new relationships with those in the community. Southside is a similar story, where members are vitally connected with the people around them as friends connecting with other friends in the name of Jesus.

The typical approach in many a church is to assume that connecting with the community and neighborhood gets people into programs designed by the church. These programs tend to reflect the needs and desires of those already attending because they are not developed through genuine engagement with people in the community. This is the genius of Southside in Vancouver. They have made a quantum leap in imagination and are creating a wealth of ways to connect with people on their own turf as friends and listeners, rather than a group with a plan and program to get people into their church building. Engaging with the communities outside the boundaries of a congregation by inviting them into programs does not lead to engagement with the community.

Leaders learn how to ask questions that invite dialogue about the shape of mission and witness in the specific places where members live and work. Mark did this when he himself suddenly realized that he was spending a great deal of his (and his family's) time driving out of the community where they lived to church meetings, to private schools, lessons for the kids, and so forth. He stopped and asked himself, *Why are we doing this?* The answers disturbed him. This question led to others. What is happening in our neighborhood? Who are our neighbors? How will we listen to them?

Mark, Nina, and the house church group read Scripture with these questions in mind. As they did, their imagination changed. They dialogued with neighbors and people in the community and started to see their area from a new perspective.

A lay leader in a presbytery we were working with expressed this reenvisioning in his attempt to "rewrite" Psalm 137 in terms of his own context:

Psalm 137 for 2010

In the midst of this crazy world I look around and wonder what
has happened. How do I talk to a kid with a ring in his nose?
Does "The Old Rugged Cross" mean anything to him?
He asks me to sing a song about "my Jesus."
From what I can tell he is from another planet,
or am I the stranger here?
I think it's time to sell the Wurlitzer.
So how do I tell Martians about Jesus, when the only
language I speak is 1955?
How do I write a headline for them
that doesn't screw up the Good News?
I kind of wish it were the way it was,
but it's not. So I need to figure out
how to sing the old lyrics
with a whole new tune.

Missional Future

In the process of understanding context and learning to ask new questions, some people (often in unexpected ways) start to develop energy for mission and ministry in their neighborhood. For example, Mike at Southside connected with school principals, and from the conversation soccer camps developed in the schools over spring break and during the summer. Creating a missional future for a church means showing and modeling for people in the church this kind of initiative and imagination.

The connections that Alan made in his church as he brought people together into coalitions of interest and energy did the same thing. As others in the congregation saw these little coalitions turn conversation into action in the neighborhood, it inspired others to come together so that new ideas and mission actions developed. Over one summer a group in the church who worked in the media wanted to connect with other media and movie business friends in the area who just wouldn't come near a church building. They came together and, in the short order of people with great imagination and organizational skills, rented a store front just down the road from the church. They opened a summer coffee house that was soon filled with the most incredible musicians who came out of the woodwork and back pews of the church eager to contribute and participate.

The more this happened, the more others began dreaming of ways to be God's people in the community. Some saw the power of actually living on the same street and turning that street into their small parish. As this happened, a missional future that no church board or small leadership group could ever plan or design took hold in the congregation. This is what is happening at Southside. It's not about strategy from the top that aligns people behind an official program. It is the energy people have to create a new future for themselves as a missional community.

A missional leader watches and listens for such gatherings of energy. They cultivate conversation and continue giving permission and encouragement for experimentation. When one group begins to engage in ministry and mission, that stimulates others' imagination, and new centers of missional energy emerge. In one sense, the leader has no control over this process. But in another sense, it cannot take place unless the leader cultivates and nurtures these centers of energy. Like a midwife, the leader encourages and challenges people in a birthing process.

Biblical Foundations *for* Change

Creating a missional congregation is a stretching, confusing experience for people. They fear the transformation means losing traditions and beliefs that have sustained them all their lives. In some ways, this is the case. It is important for leaders to connect with the biblical narratives, where God draws both Israel and the church out of their established comfort zone for them to rediscover their true purpose in being people of witness and mission in the world. The Scriptures are filled with these stories that point to a basic missional theology of being the people of God. The more these connections are made, the more people can link what they are experiencing with God's bigger story and purposes.

People wonder why we spend so much time working with Scripture when we are working with a church or denominational system. We can feel their frustration in the early stages because we keep coming back to these biblical stories. But folks want to get their money's worth, so they ask us to get quickly to the "practical" plans and actions. It takes some time before they begin to understand how critical it is to live in the biblical narratives. The denominational leaders in south Georgia wondered for a time why Alan was spending so much time with them in a passage such as Luke 10. But as this practice began challenging their assumptions about evangelism and being the church in that part of the country, they started talking to each other out of the text and challenging one another's assumptions. It was a wonderful moment.

The Bible remains the center of Christian life. The history of God's engagement with people from Adam through Abraham to Moses and then to Matthew, Paul, John, and others is meaningful in the twenty-first century. But it is wise to keep in mind that it is these stories, not doctrine or moral position, that are likely to engage the sort of people who are more attracted to *Chicken Soup for the Soul* and books by Dr. Phil than to the Bible. The challenge is in learning to communicate the biblical stories to connect with the underlying cultural narratives that dominate the lives of most of us today. The cultural narratives of fear and anxiety, loss and confusion outlined in Chapter Four are as much *inside* the community of God's people as they are *in* the neighborhoods and communities in which we live. If leaders can use the Missional Change Model of awareness, understanding, evaluation, experimentation, and commitment to encourage God's people to connect biblical narrative with their own inner story, they will cultivate the means whereby God's people can honestly engage their neighbors with the biblical stories of God's purposes.

For a traditionally trained pastor, creating this connection between biblical narrative and the life of the congregation can be challenging. In one congregation we know, the senior pastor was in denial over the extent to which the congregation tuned him out as he explained the meaning and grammatical implications of the original Greek in his sermons. All of his training in the best evangelical seminaries had predisposed him to exegete Scripture through reference to the original languages and principles of application for life. He struggled within himself with changing his preaching to focus on Scripture as story that invites people into a world where their issues are addressed not with answers about "how to make life work" but by plunging them into a new way of seeing their world.

As he tried this new and awkward way of engaging Scripture, one that lay far outside his comfort zone, people began to listen again. They started to engage with this strange world of Scripture that was opening up new questions and perspectives on their own lives. The pastor found that he was no longer providing answers; he was disrupting their world and causing them to think deeply about their own lives in the context of biblical story. As a result, many people in the congregation began discerning ways of listening to the stories of the people in their neighborhood.

Summary

This chapter has looked at some key leadership skills for working with a church in turning its energy and imagination toward engagement with the people and context in which the church finds itself. A church can lose touch with its community. It can cease listening to what is happening outside the meetings, the inner group, and the four walls of the building. The task we have laid out in this chapter describes how leaders might work with such a church in four key areas:

1. Discovering again the forces that affect the lives of people in our communities
2. Connecting people in the congregation with their neighborhood and community
3. Keeping this connection so that missional imagination about the future of the church becomes a regular part of people's thinking
4. Constantly connecting all that is happening with the biblical narratives of God's purpose.

The Spirit has been poured out in the church for the sake of the world and the kingdom. We can do no less than lead our people incarnationally into their community and neighborhood.

CHAPTER 11

Conclusion: Putting Together a Team for Leadership Development

THIS BOOK HAS PRESENTED A WAY OF UNDERSTANDING how leaders go about forming a missional congregation. How do we invite and involve leaders in the kind of change process we have outlined? At the heart of this book is the Missional Change Model.

How do pastors and leaders engage in this work? They must become apprentices in the process of *awareness* and *understanding, evaluation* and *experimentation* in order to develop *commitment* to missional leadership. At the core of this process is the leader's own readiness to risk engagement in dialogue, listening, and experimentation. In this closing chapter, we offer a brief overview of two ways in which we work with leaders to apply the thinking and practices developed in this book. They are the Pastor/Leader Survey and the Pastor/Leader Team.

The Pastor/Leader Survey

In creating a resource that could serve the process of building awareness, understanding, and evaluation, we developed a 360 degree tool that presents a comprehensive picture (what we call a "photograph") of how others see a leader's functioning across the readiness factors. Only the pastor/leader himself or herself sees the report; it can be used only to assist a leader in his or her own development by initiating awareness and creating the kind of dialogue presented in the Missional Change Model. Alongside the classic skills of preaching, pastoral care, and church management, leaders require the capacity to lead change and form a missional community. The Pastor/Leader Survey focuses on the latter skills.

The leader completes the Pastor/Leader Survey online along with fifteen to twenty-five other people the leader selects. These others receive a copy of the survey, also complete it online, and return it to our office. A fifty-page report is then created that provides rich, multifaceted feedback on how the leader is seen to be functioning with these capacities. The report, based on the sixteen readiness factors, analyzes the leader's current skill level as well as suggesting ways to identify those skills and capacities that need to be developed at this moment in their specific context.

We have discussed the framework for the readiness factors (see Chapter Six); the survey is summarized in Figure 11.1.

The survey measures the readiness factors in four areas (Table 11.1).

The power of the survey lies is in its ability to give a pastor/leader feedback from a trusted group of people who see him or her functioning in a variety of church and nonchurch settings and situations. Feedback is one of the greatest gifts a leader can receive. Unfortunately, the kind of feedback that can lead to real change and cultivation of new skills rarely takes place. In our experience pastors/leaders generally receive only two kinds: praise or blame. Either they're praised as wonderful or criticized as failing to meet people's expectations and

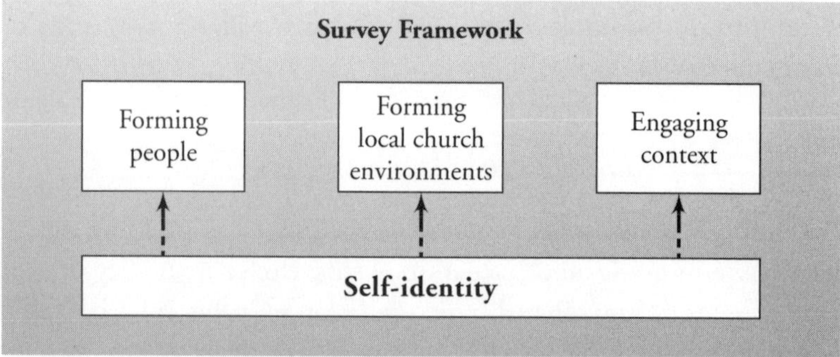

Figure 11.1. Framework for the Pastor/Leader Survey.

TABLE 11.1. *Sixteen Missional Leadership Readiness Factors.*

Missional Leadership Engagement Areas	*Required Capabilities (Readiness Factors)*
1. Self-readiness factors	1. Shows personal maturity 2. Has conflict resolution skills 3. Shows personal courage 4. Develops trust
2. People readiness factors	5. Creates missional thinking 6. Cultivates growth 7. Enables change 8. Creates coalitions
3. Congregation readiness factors	9. Fosters church integration 10. Cultivates missional culture 11. Cultivates missional practices 12. Practices missional theology
4. Community readiness factors	13. Shows understanding of our society 14. Fosters church member engagement 15. Develops missional future 16. Fosters a biblical foundation for change

needs. Neither response creates growth. The survey gives leaders a tool to see themselves as others see them in leadership at this time.

The 360 Degree Feedback Process

The 360 degree feedback process (Figure 11.2), simple and powerful, is a core feature of the survey. Quite simply, it means that the fifteen to twenty-five leaders and peers that you select complete the survey. Once compiled, their collective responses amount to a rich, in-depth photograph of how those others view you across the spectrum of readiness factors. The feedback is not prescriptive; it does not indicate what is right or wrong or how things should be in your ministry. However, it does help you to think deeply and prayerfully about your leadership. It also helps clarify how to develop leadership and where to begin the process. This photograph is the resource for you to begin the awareness-understanding-evaluation-experimentation process outlined in the second section of this chapter.

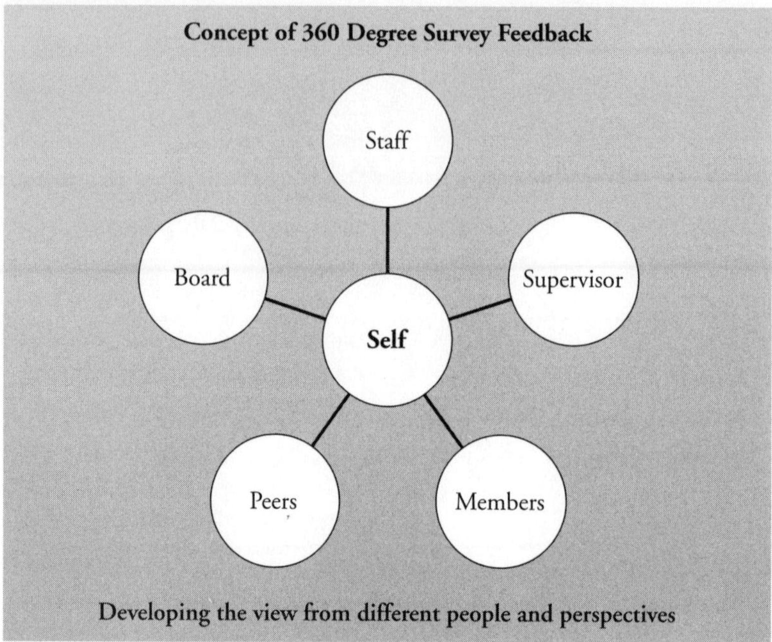

Figure 11.2. The 360 Degree Feedback Process.

The resulting feedback report is the basis for the second step: formation of a Pastor/Leader Team that is built around the survey and its feedback. The report also constitutes a guided process for designing a development plan for the subject.

It is possible to use the steps outlined in the next section of this chapter without completing the survey. A practical way to do this is by turning to the summary of readiness factors and identify one from each area that you feel represents skill and competency you want to work on. This process does not give you the critical element of feedback, which is central to the survey, but it does enable you to enter the process described in the second section, the Pastor/Leader Team.

The Pastor/Leader Team

For those wanting to develop missional leadership skills, we find that the most effective next step after the feedback report is to participate in what we call a Pastor/Leader Team. This team comprises six to eight trusted pastor/leader peers in a geographical area who will meet in a covenantal relationship over a period of twelve to eighteen months. The team is a major resource for any pastor/leader going through a major transition. We are once again learners on an uncertain journey traveling in territory that is largely unmapped. At the same time, we are also given the privilege and responsibility of oversight of a community of God's people. We cannot simply experiment with our own lives, nor the lives of those who have been entrusted to us. But we need to find a way to discover and develop skills and capacities for navigating the new landscape. How do we do both? How do we function well amid this necessary tension? The answer is simple but surprising: we need others to journey with us! What we need is a team of peers who are willing to take the risk of becoming a learning community committed to calling forth the best in one another.

It is unusual for pastors and leaders in the church to become part of a team where the purpose is to work on mutual development of the skills and capacities required to be effective missional leaders. We have found that these teams are critical in this process of identifying the skills and capacities requisite to work in our ministry situation. Teams discover the power of working with and for one another in forming new leadership capacities and addressing the real-life challenges each leader confronts in a specific congregation. This section outlines how to form such a team. It lays out the details of regular monthly meetings and how they enable you to form a development plan. We present this process to show you a way of moving forward in discerning the skills and capacities for innovating missional change in your context.

Figure 11.3 summarizes the overall process we have developed. Across the top of the diagram are the five stages of the Missional Change Model. The survey and feedback report are part of the awareness and understanding stages. Following these stages, the Pastor/Leader Team is formed and designed to set a context for the evaluation stage. Out of the team work described in this section comes the experimentation stage, where we use a tool called the Missional Action Team (MAT). This process takes the development plan that the pastor/leaders have put together in their team and indicates in practical terms how to put the plan into action. In this way, at every step the pastor/leaders participating in a team are learning from their own experience how to work with the MCM. This action-learning process prepares them to engage their own local churches with the model.

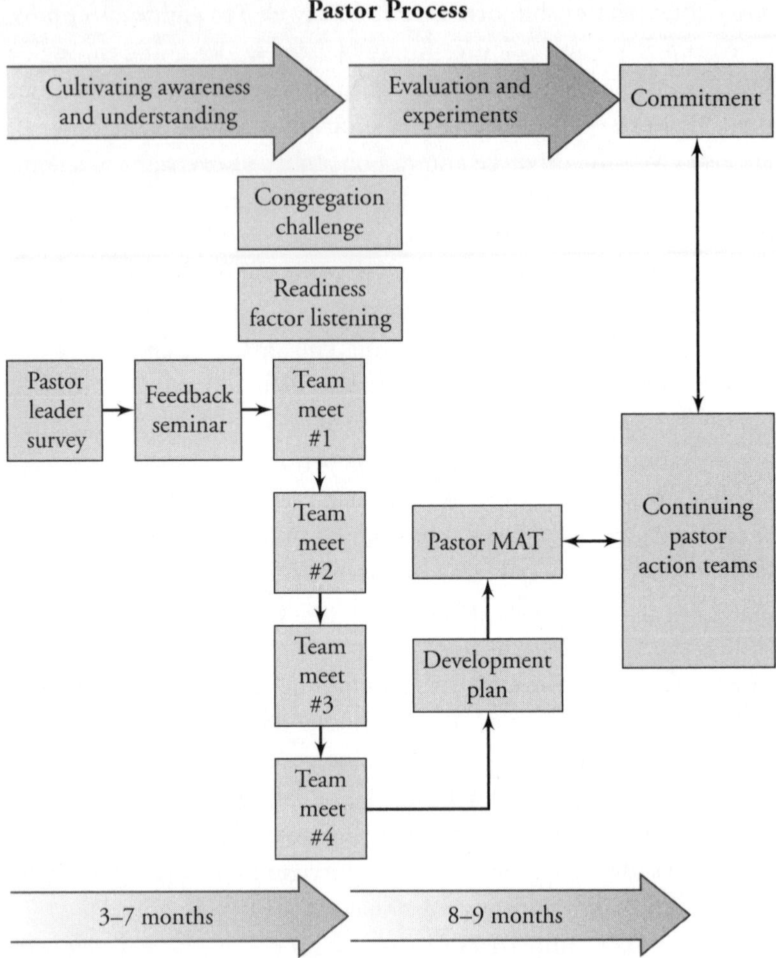

Figure 11.3. An Overview of the Pastor/Leader Team Process.

The bottom of Figure 11.3 suggests an approximate timeline for each stage. The team process outlined here describes the first five to seven months of the process, where the team works with their report to (1) identify the specific readiness factors team members want to work on and (2) engage in a listening process to deepen their understanding of the factors and evaluate the meaning of people's feedback for their leadership development. The stages that follow the development plan take a further eight or nine months of working with the Missional Action Team process.

Pastor/Leader Team: The First Five to Seven Months

These are the steps for the first time period:

1. Complete the Pastor/Leader Survey.
2. Receive the survey report and attend a feedback session to understand the report.
3. Form the Pastor/Leader Team with a group of five to eight leaders who have also taken the survey and been to a feedback seminar.
4. In this team, over the next five or six months do three things:

    Identify one readiness factor from each engagement area. Use these factors to engage in a series of listening conversations where you ask others for feedback and use that feedback to deepen your own understanding of how the chosen factors are seen to be operating in you at this point.

    Identify a significant adaptive, missional leadership challenge you must address in your local church if you are to lead this community toward missional change.

    Commit to following a set of practices of Christian life as a team of leaders.

5. On the basis of the work in step four, team members assist each other to design a personal leadership development plan. At this point the team moves to the stage of implementing the plan in the congregation (this final stage is not shown in this chapter).

The Value of the Pastor/Leader Team

Alan and one of his associates, Pat, once had a conference call with a group of denomination executives who were wondering why they had to talk together about what they were learning. Pat suddenly commented to one of the executives: "Bill, experience teaches you nothing!" There was a long silence. It sounded like a statement out of left field. No one knew what to say in response because it sounded so counterintuitive. Of course we learn by experience; or that's what we've all been taught. Then Pat went on: "The only experience we learn from is the experience we reflect upon, and to do that we need others who will assist us in the reflection."

It is only with trusted peers that we effectively reflect upon our experience as a leader and wrestle with what we are doing and the challenges we face. Creating leadership development teams is an important element of the new missional leadership paradigm. In them pastor/leaders discover the power of working with and for one another in both forming new capacities and addressing the real-life challenges of their congregation. Almost every pastor we work with nods in agreement when we say that the *sola pastora* model of leadership is killing pastors; more often than not it leads to terrible discouragement and loneliness and creates a deep sense of personal failure. But few know what to do about it. There are many reasons that these deep-seated and chronic problems at the heart of local church leadership have not been addressed. A few common ones follow, but you can probably add your own as well.

- Pastors have been schooled to think and act in a *sola pastora* way.
- We don't know of any other models to look at and emulate. Business and management models don't really work; nor do we see any others that apply.
- We are reluctant to trust ourselves to others. We are afraid of being known for who we are and how we function as a leader—unless we have real success stories to share with others. Our theology says that we should lead from below, but all our models say we should look and act successful.
- We are afraid that the congregation will be resistant to our spending time with a pastor team talking about the congregation.
- We would not know what to do if we formed such a team. We don't have any models for how we can be together to reflect on our experiences and learn and grow.

A Pastor/Leader team can combat these distressing trends; this is why we developed this team process. A team comprises people within a geographic area (within the same city, or perhaps within less than a one-hour drive from a central meeting location). Members are committed to their own and one another's development in missional leadership.

The Basics of a Pastor/Leader Team

The five-to-eight-member Pastor/Leader Team meets for four to six months. At the end of that time, each team member creates a development plan and becomes ready to move to the Missional Action Team phase (MAT, not discussed in this chapter but seen in Figure 11.3). The team works together to deepen awareness and understanding of key leadership skills that each person needs to develop. These are the goals of the team:

- Assist in understanding each other's specific readiness factors.
- Practice together a set of disciplines for forming missional life among pastors/leaders. The team identifies these disciplines and commits to keeping them over the life of the team.
- Work together at forming each other's missional leadership development plan.

To effectively work at these three levels, the team's first task is to develop a covenant. This creates the framework for working together and includes a number of provisions:

1. Attend each monthly meeting.

   Commit five to six hours of your time to each monthly meeting.

   Check your calendar to set dates and keep the commitment.
2. Practice strict confidentiality.

   Everything shared in a meeting is done in complete confidentiality.

   Sharing outside the group can occur only with prior agreement among all members.
3. Faithfully engage in the agreed practices.

   Identify two or three practices of Christian life you agree to apply over the coming four months, such as keeping the daily office twice per day, praying for one another regularly, and providing hospitality to the stranger once per month.

Decide the frequency of these practices and the means of reporting to one another.

4. Give a truthful accounting of your engagement.

   Part of the journey in awareness and understanding is to reflect honestly on how you are listening and managing the practices you are doing month by month as a team. Only in honest truth telling is there real development and growth.

5. Pray with and for one another regularly.

   It is God who shapes and calls forth the missional leadership we require. The process you are engaged in does not presume that we can predefine how you will determine your leadership in the days ahead. As you walk in prayer, you will discern God's direction for you.

Elements of Each Development Team Meeting

The first element of a development team meeting is to *engage Scripture.* Scripture is a central element in forming missional leadership. Each meeting begins with a period of indwelling Scripture. This is not formal Bible study, nor is it showing our prowess in exegesis. Instead, it involves gathering together around a series of simple questions that ask how God is addressing us in the passage. Briefly, these are the stages:

1. Read the text together. (Luke 10:1–12 is the one we use every time we meet. We don't move from text to text but live in this one text every time.)
2. Remain in silence, asking yourself where the text caught you, where you stopped in the passage, and how God might be speaking to you out of this listening.
3. Turn to another member of the team and briefly (two minutes each) share your response to the passage.
4. In the whole group, each member speaks and the others listen.

The second element is to *announce listening engagement.* Over this period, team members are engaged in a series of listening experiences around their readiness factors. In the team meetings, each person relates what he or she is hearing and learning in these engagements.

Third is to *cultivate practices.* Declare how you have done in living out the practices you agreed to attend to.

Fourth is to *tell your congregation leadership story.* You listen to and engage each other around the congregational stories each team member is writing month by month. This process assists each person in identifying the missional leadership challenge to be addressed in the congregation.

Fifth is to *debrief.* We learn by reflecting on our experience. At the end of each meeting, the team reflects on what has happened in the meeting and what worked and what did not, to practice the skills of reflection and making a successful team work.

Agenda for the First Three Meetings

The meeting begins by engaging Scripture (thirty minutes).

Next comes formation of triads for listening feedback (forty-five minutes). In this section of the meeting, the team meets in groups of three to give each member ten to fifteen minutes for reporting on the feedback from his or her listening processes during the prior month. The other two members provide feedback by asking questions that seek to clarify and deepen the understanding of the one reporting. This is not a time for developing strategies or looking at action solutions but instead to continue listening. Triad time lays the groundwork for the fourth meeting, in which the development plan is confirmed.

In whole team feedback (thirty minutes), the team as a whole uses this time to catch up on what they have been doing during the past month as well as relate a little of what they have been learning.

Next is reporting on practices (forty-five minutes). Asking each group member to report on practices, the team checks in with one another to discover what they have been learning as well as to be accountable for their commitments.

Sharing of church stories is then carried out in triads (forty-five minutes). In this period of four months, the team works on identifying a primary leadership challenge that each leader has in the congregation. In the first two meetings, each member is invited to describe the story of the congregation in a brief presentation. The purpose of the storytelling is to understand the nature of the leadership challenges the pastor needs to address in his or her congregation. Other team members are invited to ask awareness-and-understanding questions. At the end of the third meeting, each team member identifies what he or she believes is the leadership challenge to be addressed in context.

Homework and assignments are next (fifteen minutes). As the team agrees, there is ongoing work, research, or planning that needs to be carried out between meetings. This is the time to assign and clarify work to be done.

Finally, there is a debrief (thirty minutes). At the end of each meeting there is a brief time for feedback on what was helpful and not-so-helpful in the meeting. We learn only by reflecting on our experience.

Preparation for the Team Meetings

There are three areas where team members prepare for each meeting: identifying the readiness factors they will focus on, engaging in the listening process to deepen understanding, and developing the story of one's leadership in this congregation.

The next few pages are helpful in focusing reflection and preparation on the team meeting.

IDENTIFY READINESS FACTORS TO FOCUS ON. Prior to the first team meeting, identify up to four readiness factors to use over the coming months of Pastor/Leader Team meetings. These are factors you use to deepen your understanding of your current leadership; they are based on use of the Pastor/Leader Survey. You might also simply reflect on the factors outlined in Chapters Eight through Ten and then select a factor from each area. It is obviously better to do the survey, but an alternative method gives you at least a sense of how the team works.

This is an important first step. We ask each pastor/leader to set aside time to review survey results given in the report and use the questions presented here to select no more than four readiness factors to be explored, with the team, in depth during the months ahead.

- What are your high readiness factor scores?
- How would you assess these factors as representing the skills, strengths, and resources you bring to leadership?
- Which readiness factor scores seem most critical for you to develop?
- Which readiness factor scores surprise you the most?
- Which scores concern you the most?
- What are you most concerned about with these specific factors?

Using these questions, select the four readiness factors you will work on in the team in the months ahead. You should choose factors that:

- Build on your strengths
- You believe are important rather than what someone else may want you to focus on
- You believe are feasible for you to develop in twelve to eighteen months

At the first team meeting, each member identifies the four readiness factors selected along with a brief comment on the reasons. Each member also presents a list of these factors so everyone has a record for reference and ongoing discussion. In this way, the entire team is involved with people's choices as the basis for the team's work in the months ahead.

BETWEEN TEAM MEETINGS, ENGAGE IN LISTENING CONVERSATION. The second part of the team process involves identifying a group of people to meet with over the four months, to interview them about the readiness factors you have selected. The rationale and process for meeting with these people is described here, but the basic reason for these meetings is to deepen your understanding of the four readiness factors you have selected. The listening process we invite you into takes time. It involves meeting with selected people and carefully paying attention to what they have to say. This is how the gift of feedback is deepened. By taking the time to listen, you move deeper in your awareness and understanding of what the survey report is indicating about the readiness factors you've chosen. This listening process continues through the first three or four months of Pastor/Leader Team meetings. You need that much time to gather the data to design your development plan. Here are the steps for setting up the listening interviews that gather feedback on the four readiness factors you have selected.

First, identify six to eight people who know you relatively well and whose insights and advice you trust. These people should be selected from (1) those who have completed the survey for you, (2) other peers in leadership, (3) members of your local church, and (4) other members of your leadership team.

Here are some characteristics to look for in the selection process:

- You trust their confidentiality.
- You respect their input.
- They can present objective feedback.
- They see you as neither a hero nor a demon but have a healthy perspective on your leadership.
- They will not use this information in any negative way.
- They have the ability to reflect on actions and connect ideas.
- Everyone is given a clear rationale for the interview.

Here is a script for how you might do that:

> I'm calling you with a request because I respect your insight and wisdom. I would like an hour of your time to listen to your input on a number of aspects of my leadership. I am committed to becoming the best leader for this congregation I can possibly become.
>
> To this end, I have taken a Missional Leader Readiness Survey. About twelve to fifteen people filled out this survey on me (you may have been one of them). Some of the scores have been very encouraging, but some areas are going to need my attention. I now want to spend several weeks listening to trusted people in order to develop a better understanding of my scores in several areas. I would be honored if you were willing to let me interview you about these scores.

> I want to show you four of my scores and ask you for your reflections on them. I will ask you about how you have observed actions that might have resulted in the score I received. I want to just listen to what you have to say, take notes, and perhaps ask a few clarification questions. But my overall purpose in this interview is to listen to you. I don't want you to be artificial or just say nice things. I really want the feedback to learn and grow from this process. After the listening is completed, I am going to put together a development plan to grow in my leadership. So I need real feedback from you.

In terms of the interviews themselves, it's important to provide a clear structure and observe a few basic rules of behavior. You will also want to make sure that you can capture the feedback you receive.

Before the interview:

- Establish an interview schedule over a six-to-twelve-week period in which you can comfortably carry out six to eight interviews.
- Phone each person several weeks ahead of time.
- Explain why you are calling and state the amount of time you are asking for (no more than one hour per interview).
- Set up a time and place for the meeting. (It should always be face-to-face.)
- Make sure the location is quiet and you will not be interrupted for the hour.
- Photocopy the four pages of the readiness factors you have identified from the survey report and have been working with for the meeting.

At the interview:

- Arrive early to make sure the location is well set up.
- Keep your cell phone off.
- Have a notebook available for note taking. Do not use a portable computer; the screen will isolate you from the other person.

- Greet the individual; thank him or her for giving you this time.
- Review the purpose of the meeting, and explain again what you want to accomplish.
- Show the person the four pages of the survey, and reiterate your desire for honest feedback.
- Listen, listen, listen! Ask only clarification questions so that you are certain you understand what is being said. Take brief notes that will help you remember key elements of the conversation.

A few cautions for the interview:

- Don't try to explain why you did something.
- Don't get caught up in offering details of an action or event. Keep the focus on listening.
- Watch the other person's body language and your own; a gasp, pause, or raised voice can communicate anxiety that tends to shut down communication.
- Don't let the interview go more than fifty minutes. Keep your time commitment to the individual.
- If you are meeting in a restaurant, insist that you pay the bill for the meal.
- Thank the individual again for having taken a risk and probably saying some things that were hard to say. Let the person know he or she has been heard, that this has been an important meeting, and that you are very grateful for the feedback.

After the interview:

• Immediately find a quiet place and write a detailed verbatim rendering of the interview. This is an important way to deepen the listening and make sure you have actually internalized what was said. We encourage people to keep a journal devoted to writing on every interview.

• E-mail or send a written thank-you note to the individual, or simply make a phone call. Review your listening and try to summarize what you have heard in four or five main points.

• Identify additional listening and clarification questions to ask the next person on the basis of the last interview.

In the Pastor/Leader Team meetings, members report what they are hearing and learning from these interviews and receive feedback from team members. Everyone should make sure to complete all the interviews before the third Pastor/Leader Team meeting.

DEVELOP THE STORY OF YOUR LEADERSHIP IN THE LOCAL CHURCH. Prior to the first Pastor/Leader Team meeting, look over and familiarize yourself with these twelve questions. Write a brief response to the first four questions prior to meeting one, the next four prior to meeting two, and the final four for meeting three. During team meetings, each member is invited to present his or her story while other members ask questions as a means of providing feedback. The purpose is to assist you in identifying one of the primary missional leadership challenges you need to address in your congregation.

Write an autobiography of your leadership in your current congregation. This is a brief history of your involvement in the congregation from the perspective of being a primary leader. Focus on the leadership you are addressing as well as your own responses to those leadership issues. Use this numbered outline to write your history:

1. Give a brief historical account of your involvement in the congregation, including a chronological list of times and events from a leadership perspective.
2. Describe your assessment of the character and ethos of the congregation.
3. What are the primary metaphors that currently shape the imagination and language of the congregation?
4. How would you describe the congregation's understanding of its own story?
5. Summarize your most significant leadership experiences.
6. How might the congregation write the history of your leadership among them?

7. What are the major biblical passages or themes that currently inform your understanding of (1) the congregation and (2) your leadership?
8. What are the two major events that have influenced your leadership in this congregation, and how would you assess them now?
9. Reflect on your experience of leadership in this congregation and the most significant experiences that affected you as a child and teenager.
10. What were the most significant experiences (one or two) of wounding and healing in your life?
11. What have been the major developments in your ecclesiology over the past five years? How has this affected your understanding and practice of leadership?
12. What do you see as the two or three primary leadership challenges you must address in forming a missional congregation in this place?

Preparing *for the* Final Pastor/Leader Team Meeting

The final Pastor/Leader Team meeting is where you bring together all that you have learned. Following the third meeting, set aside half a day to complete the reflection process that follows here. The purpose is to take all the feedback you have received from both your listening and the team's reflections and develop a tentative description of your missional leadership development plan.

Reflection Process

Prior to the final team meeting, create a one-page summary of your learning for each factor you have chosen (four pages in total). Reflect on these summaries through these questions:

- What are some potential options to developing skills and capacities in each of these four Factors?

- Which potential options best address the challenges of an adaptive change in your leadership? Which are a more technical response? Do you need a combination of both? If so, what might that combination look like for you?
- What resources (people, financial, time, travel) are required for the options you are exploring?
- What would be involved in implementing these options right now?
- Who will be affected, and how?
- What might be some potential reactions from people?
- Which options will you select, and how will you give a rationale to the people who need to confirm these decisions with you?

The Leadership Challenge

Write one or two paragraphs that respond to this statement: "In my current congregation a primary leadership challenge I will address over the next twelve months is. . . ." In light of this challenge statement, reflect on these questions:

- What are the potential ways you know of responding to this challenge?
- What are the skills and capacities you need to address this challenge?
- What are the action steps you might develop to engage this challenge in the coming months?
- Who are the other leaders in the congregation who can be your allies in developing and initiating a plan to engage this challenge?
- What are the important communication steps needed to effect this leadership challenge?
- Who will be affected by this challenge if you engage it in the church right now?
- How will various groups feel an impact?
- What are the implementation obstacles for you personally?

- What are the implementation obstacles within the congregation?
- What will be the short-term and long-term impact of your working on this leadership challenge?
- What can be done to minimize potential reaction to addressing this leadership challenge?

From this reflective work, you are now ready to complete the information that follows, which is then brought to your team. At the team meeting you present these plans to one another to receive further feedback and confirmation.

Proposed Action Plan

Outline the action steps you plan to take for (1) the skills and capacities and (2) the leadership challenge you have identified. Create two separate proposals based on this template:

- Skills and capacities (or leadership challenge) I have identified to work on: ___________
- Who needs to be involved, and what are their roles?
- What is the key message you want to communicate to these people, and how will you do so?
- What media and materials might you want to use to develop an effective communication process with them? Write an outline of your intended communication.
- Outline the timelines and benchmarks that will guide these actions.
- List the resources required with a clear indication of cost, responsibility, and time commitment.
- Develop a presentation that effectively communicates your development plan to your leadership in the congregation

Final Team Meeting

At the final team meeting, each member shares the action plan to receive feedback from other members.

At the conclusion of this final meeting, team members evaluate what they have learned, working as a team, as to their own development and then explore how they might continue working with one another as their plans are implemented in each congregation. The team then has the option to continue as their plans are being worked through over the next six months.

Conclusion

We have taken a long journey together in this book. This conclusion is being written very early in the morning, as Alan flies across the country after spending three days working with the faculty of a seminary and then a team of a dozen pastors on the leadership frameworks developed in this book.

The faculty is unique among seminaries in North America; it is intentionally asking questions about the formation of leaders for the emerging missional environment. But this is not just a conversation in the Practical Theology Department. The whole faculty, across all its disciplines, is participating in the conversation and putting together a series of actions to develop alternative approaches to training and curriculum.

A comment from a member of the theology department was striking. Todd told the other faculty members that as a theologian he found himself in a place of *transition* as he sought to understand how to form leaders with a missional imagination. The core ideas of this book are now assisting this entire faculty in thinking through the question of leadership formation and training of missional leaders.

At the same time, a dozen pastors, invited by the seminary, are participating in the process outlined in this chapter as they implement the frameworks of change we have introduced in the body of this book. Teams of this kind are working together now in various places across North America and in Australia. As one pastor in Pittsburgh said to the board of his denomination, "This understanding of leadership and the process of development we have been given has re-energized and changed my whole understanding and practice of ministry." The executive minister of that denomination said the teams we've described in this chapter and the frameworks of leadership development we've introduced in this book are among the most important skills he's been given in many years of leadership.

But our journey in shaping the ideas and practices in this book did not come easily or quickly. Neither of us started our work as a leader (one in the business world, the other in the church world) with the frameworks presented here. Indeed, for a long time they seemed counterintuitive and contrary to many of our own ideas and practices of leadership. It took years to gradually understand that there was a way of leading to genuinely engage the core reality of the church—that the Spirit of God is among the people of God and therefore the answer to the questions of the church's missional life in particular places is among the people. Leadership is about cultivating the kind of environment that frees God's people to feel again the winds of the Spirit and to sail the holy gusts of the Spirit's directions in waters where we no longer have good, clear, definitive maps. The freedom and energy that came from these discoveries was immense for each of us and changed almost everything we had come to believe about leadership in the church.

Many years ago, Alan took up windsurfing. It was the kind of sport that, once you learn the skills, allows you to fly across the water, catching winds and experiencing the exhilaration of surfing the edge of the wave. But developing the skills required a learning curve that was counterintuitive. Soon after purchasing his first surfboard, he went on a three-week family vacation to a camp ground in Ontario that lay beside a wonderfully long lake.

Each afternoon, as the wind came up, he would string the mast, set up the board, and start the learning process (lessons were deemed unnecessary, and the instruction book he purchased was a quick read that didn't penetrate deeply into his eager mind). The first task was to learn balance while simply standing on the board in relatively calm water. Next came the work of lifting the mast out of the water, holding it upright to the wind, and still keeping balance on the board. These stages took a few days of focused work, but it was vacation time and there were adventures to be had out there on the lake. He was eager to get up and out into the real water where the wind was blowing away from the land. About a week into these learning rituals, it began to feel as if everything was coming together: the balance was there, the sail skills seemed to be coming along well. He could now move out a little from shore, turn around, and come back into the camp without falling too many times. It felt as if the basic training was complete and a little adventure was in order.

One afternoon around 4:30, Alan took the board out onto the lake. The wind was light but just enough to move him forward and create a nice ripple across his board as he moved. The sail was easy to handle. The world was good! What he didn't understand yet (there were a good many things he did not yet understand about windsurfing at this point) was the relationship between wind and land on a lake. Basically, the land adjacent to a lake pushes the main wind up high, so that when one is on the water within a few hundred yards of land the wind feels quite minimal and manageable. But more than a few hundred yards out on the water the land effect disappears, and the full force of the wind is felt at water level. He discovered that the further out he went the more the wind picked up, until he felt himself, for the first time, catching the winds and sailing at a rate he never expected. He quickly learned to lean way back on the board in order to balance and hold onto the sail, which now felt as if it wanted to rip itself out of his grip. He was flying across the lake; it was a huge, adrenalin rush, a great blast. Here is what life was made for, this incredible run across the water.

Within twenty minutes he was on the other side of the lake, sitting on another beach, catching his breath, and exulting in the conquest of water. It was now getting toward 6:00 P.M. and time for him to head back to the camp to join the rest of the family in cooking dinner and enjoying an evening around the campfire. This would be an evening for stories; the adventure had begun and there was still a huge amount of the lake to conquer in the days ahead. After getting on the board, he turned it toward the camp to head home. He was ready now for the wind, but what happened was totally outside how he anticipated the return trip.

As soon as he hit the wind the sail caught and suddenly flung him head over heels into the water. Confused, he climbed up onto the board and started all over again, hoisting the sail and pointing the board straight toward the camp. It was a direct line; he could see the camp faintly in the distance, so it shouldn't have been too difficult to just aim the board in that direction and head home. But the wind and the board weren't going to operate according to his mind map of reality.

Time after time, he would point the board to the camp and be flung into the water head-first. He was getting mad; no board is going to do that to him. He was also getting very confused: Why did this keep happening? What was wrong? Why couldn't he just head home?

As confusion shifted toward concern and exhaustion started to shake his now-cold body, Alan discovered something that was completely counterintuitive for him at that point: the only way he could sail the board into the wind and stay up was to let it move in a direction that was 90–100 degrees away from the camp.

As this happened, it slowly dawned on him that when you are sailing you have to tack with the wind; you can't follow a straight line to get to where you want to go. But it all felt so strange and contrary to everything he knew about getting things done and achieving goals.

Slowly, he moved off, away from the camp. Slowly he turned the sail in the opposite direction, and slowly he edged toward the camp . . . several hours away.

In the days that followed, Alan experimented with this new, counterintuitive understanding of sailing. As he did so, he gradually came to feel and sense the winds and gusts as they blew up and down and across the lake. These new skills began to take hold, and as they did so the real adventuring began: sailing the gusts of the lake, flying across the water with a joy and abandon that gives life.

The principles and skills developed in this book feel to many leaders totally counterintuitive, but we have seen how, when they enter upon this journey of cultivating an environment that calls forth the winds of the Spirit among the people of God, they discover for themselves how to sail the holy gusts of the Spirit's life. May you enter the adventure and discover the winds of the Spirit blowing through your people.

Notes

Chapter Two

1. For a more detailed discussion of these metaphors, see chapter seven of *Missional Church: A Vision for the Sending of the Church in North America* (Grand Rapids, Mich.: Eerdmans, 1998), edited by Darrell Guder; and Alan Roxburgh's *The Missionary Congregation, Leadership, Liminality* (Harrisburg, Pa.: Trinity Press International, 1998).
2. Zygmunt Bauman, *Society Under Siege* (Cambridge, UK: Polity Press, 2002), p. 30.
3. Robert Putnam, *Bowling Alone in America* (New York: Simon and Schuster, 2001).

Chapter Three

1. It is interesting that a lot of people are working with ideas similar to this model in an attempt to describe a more organic and system-shaped approach to the changes that need to occur in organizations. One rich discussion is in David K. Hurst's *Crisis and Renewal: Meeting the Challenge of Organizational Change* (Boston: Harvard Business School Press, 2002). For those who wish to read more widely on the background to this kind of model, Hurst's material is very helpful.
2. Steven Johnson, *Emergence* (New York: Penguin, 2001), p. 18.
3. Richard Pascale, Mark Millemann, and Linda Gioja, *Surfing the Edge of Chaos* (New York: Random House, 2001), pp. 113–114.

Chapter Four

1. Ulrich Beck, *Democracy Without Enemies* (Cambridge, Mass.: Polity Press, 1998), p. 10.
2. Beck (1998), pp. 10–11.
3. Beck (1998), p. 20.

4. Zygmunt Bauman, *In Search of Politics* (Cambridge, Mass.: Polity Press, 2000), p. 2.
5. Bauman (2000), pp. 64–65.
6. For a brilliant, extended discourse on this essential need in our culture, see George Steiner's magisterial work, *Real Presences* (Chicago: University of Chicago Press, 1989).
7. Alasdair MacIntyre, *After Virtue* (Notre Dame, Ind.: Notre Dame Press, 1984). See chapter fifteen, where he argues that selfhood is a "concept of a self whose unity resides in the unity of a narrative which links birth to life to death as narrative" (p. 205). "Narrative history of a certain kind turns out to be the basic and essential genre for the characterization of human actions" (p. 208).
8. MacIntyre (1984), p. 216.
9. Jenny Rankin, "What Is Narrative? Ricoeur, Bakhtin, and Process Approaches." *Concrescence: The Australasian Journal of Process Thought,* 2002, *3,* p. 1.

Chapter Five

1. Ron Heifetz, "A Survival Guide for Leaders." *HBR,* June 2002, p. 68.
2. Joseph J. Ellis, *The Founding Brothers* (New York: Vintage, 2000).
3. Ellis (2000), p. 5.
4. Ellis (2000), p. 216.
5. Ellis (2000), p. 248.

Chapter Six

1. Those who, for example, worked as a writing team on the book from the Gospel and Our Culture Network *Treasure in Clay Jars* (Lois Y. Barrett and others, editors; Grand Rapids, Mich.: Eerdmans, 2003) made a deliberate choice not to use the word *leader* because of their conviction that it was highly problematic in terms of describing the particular forms of Christian charisms that participate in the formation of men and women as witnessing communities of the kingdom. The authors have some sympathy with these concerns, but the word is used and explained throughout the text with the belief that, like so many other words currently in use in church life (for example, salvation), it is better to address the problem and work with the language than to introduce more complex and cumbersome language forms to express what is intended.
2. Wayne Meeks, *The Origins of Christian Morality: The First Two Centuries* (New Haven, Conn.: Yale University Press, 1993) p. 26.
3. Alan Kreider, *The Change of Conversion and the Origin of Christendom* (Harrisburg, Pa.: Trinity Press International, 1999).
4. Kreider (1999), p. 90.
5. See D. Stephen Long, *The Goodness of God* (Grand Rapids, Mich.: Brazos Press, 2001) for an extended argument on how ethics is separated from theology.
6. Lesslie Newbigin, *Proper Confidence* (Grand Rapids, Mich.: Eerdmans, 1995).

7. See Kreider (1999).
8. Stanley Hauerwas, *After Christendom?* (Nashville, Tenn.: Abingdon, 1991), p. 97.
9. Hauerwas (1991), p. 107.
10. This is surely an element of David J. Bosch's argument in *Transforming Mission: Paradigm Shifts in Theology of Mission* (Maryknoll, N.Y.: Orbis, 1991) when he describes the work of the Spirit in Acts as that of boundary breaking. The point is that the Spirit breaks in and reveals an alternative imagination from that planned, expected, and strategized by the leaders of Jerusalem and elsewhere. This implies that modern notions of strategy and control impose upon the life of the ecclesia a false set of frameworks that can lead it only away from being the sign, foretaste, and witness of the kingdom irrespective of how successful such actions may be in building large congregations.

Chapter Seven

1. Robert W. Terry, *Authentic Leadership: Courage in Action* (San Francisco: Jossey-Bass, 1993), p. 113.
2. See Eugene Peterson, *A Long Obedience in the Same Direction* (Grand Rapids, Mich.: Eerdmans, 1985).

Chapter Eight

1. Elizabeth O'Conner, *Journey Inward, Journey Outward* (San Francisco: Harper, 1968); *Call to Commitment* (New York: Harper & Row, 1963).
2. Kenneth Gergen, *The Saturated Self: The Dilemmas of Identity in Contemporary Society* (New York: Basic Books, 1991).
3. They used a small guidebook. See David Adam, *The Rhythm of Life* (Harrisburg, Pa.: Morehouse, 1997).
4. See Patrick Keifert, *Welcoming the Stranger.* St. Paul, Minn.: Augsburg/Fortress, 1992).
5. See Richard Sennet, *The Fall of Public Man: On the Social Psychology of Capitalism* (New York: Random House, 1978).

Acknowledgments

So many people justly deserve their names on this page. Every author recognizes he or she stands on the shoulders of a huge crowd of partners and fellow travelers from the past and in the present. Thank you to all those people who put their trust and confidence in me when others viewed me as a nuisance or threat.

I thank Wally Mills, who, many years ago, saw a rough teenager through God's eyes and drew him into the kingdom; I am eternally grateful.

I thank my older brother, Robert, who was like a compass for me through many years.

Sheryl Fullerton and the staff of Jossey-Bass made this book what it is today; they are a great team.

The partnership of Paul and John in Melbourne, Australia, was important to the development of this book, and I will be always grateful for their friendship.

Books of this kind are formed on the road, through engagements with all sorts of people in hundreds of congregations and denominational systems. The ability to travel so much and to so many places rests on the support and love of my wife, Jane. She is on every page of this book. After all the traveling is done, she is the one who most embodies this kind of leadership.

About the Authors

Alan J. Roxburgh is a pastor, teacher, writer, and consultant with more than thirty years' experience in church leadership, consulting, and seminary education. Home is Vancouver, Canada, where he lives with his wife, Jane, a high school principal. He has pastored congregations in a small town, the suburbs, and the redevelopment of a downtown urban church as well as the planting of other congregations. He has directed an urban training center focused on seminary graduates for cross-cultural ministry in Canada and overseas, as well as serving as a seminary professor and director of a center for mission and evangelism. He teaches as an adjunct professor in seminaries in the United States, Australia, and Europe. His books include *Reaching a New Generation*; *Leadership, Liminality and the Missionary Congregation*; *Crossing the Bridge: Leadership in a Time of Change*; and *The Sky Is Falling: Leaders Lost in Transition.* He was a member of the writing team that authored *Missional Church: A Vision for the Sending of the Church in North America.*

Roxburgh is currently working with the Allelon Missional Leadership Network in the formation of leaders for the missional church. He leads conferences and seminars with denominations, congregations, and seminaries across North America, Australia, and the United Kingdom as well as consulting with these groups in the areas of leadership for missional transformation and methods of system transformation.

He has been a leader in the Gospel and Our Culture Network as well as managing a GOCN-Lilly Endowment research project into innovation of missional systems.

When not traveling or writing, he enjoys mountain biking, hiking, cooking, and hanging out with Jane and the grandchildren, as well as drinking great coffee in the Pacific Northwest.

Fred Romanuk brings more than twenty-five years of organizational consulting experience to the Missional Leadership Institute. He holds a doctorate in clinical and organizational psychology from York University, in Toronto. He studied at London Bible College in London, Ontario, and comes from an Anabaptist background. He has been involved in both Baptist and Mennonite Brethren churches.

Romanuk has worked with large national and international organizations in management of change. He built a consulting firm and directed the organization practice of a large international consulting firm for Canada and for the eastern region of the United States, working out of Baltimore, Maryland. He has led major strategic planning initiatives for Panasonic in New Jersey; Hoechst Celanese in Montreal; British Electricity International in London, UK; the Canadian Gas Association in Toronto; the United Way in Ottawa; and many other organizations in Canada and the United States.

As a psychologist, he has worked with senior executives in assessing and developing the capabilities of people in leadership roles.

Index

D

E